UNDERSTANDING CONGREGATIONS

MOWBRAY PARISH HANDBOOKS:

An ABC for the PCC: A Handbook for Church Council Members, *3rd edition*
John Pitchford

Appointed for Growth: A Handbook for Ministry Development and Appraisal
Kevin Eastell (ed.)

Community Work: A Handbook for Volunteer Groups and Local Churches
Malcolm Grundy

Handbook for Churchwardens and Parochial Church Councillors, *1997 edition*
Kenneth M. Macmorran, Timothy Briden

Learning for Life: A Handbook of Adult Religious Education
Yvonne Craig

Spring into Action: A Handbook of Local Fundraising
Martin Field and Alison Whyte (eds)

Yours, Lord: A Handbook of Christian Stewardship
Michael Wright

UNDERSTANDING CONGREGATIONS

*A new shape for the
local church*

Malcolm Grundy

MOWBRAY

Mowbray
A Cassell imprint
Wellington House, 125 Strand, London WC2R 0BB
370 Lexington Avenue, New York, NY 10017-6550
www.cassell.co.uk

First published 1998

British Library Cataloguing-in-Publication Data
A catalogue record for this book is available from the British Library.

ISBN 0-264-67482-0

Designed and typeset by Kenneth Burnley in Irby, Wirral, Cheshire.
Printed and bound in Great Britain by Biddles Ltd, Guildford and
King's Lynn.

This book is dedicated to my parents,
Arthur James Grundy
and
Gertrude Alice Grundy

Part of the fabric of one village congregation

Contents

Preface

In order to write this book at all I have been challenged, educated – and bruised – by the experiences of being a parish priest, a trainer of laity and clergy and a consultant to a range of religious and voluntary organizations. The people who became my friends and colleagues have taught and inspired me as I have tried to work out for myself how Christian groups fit into a wider society. I am still searching, questioning and learning. Much of what I have tried to put together in this book has been given to me by others who are on a similar quest. There will also be many connections for those who are now looking at how to continue the development of their congregations following an Alpha Course or a deepening-of-faith course such as Emmaus.

My thanks must go to the Edward King Institute for Ministry Development for all the stimulation and support which its members and directors have given me over the many years of my association with them. My particular thanks also go to the EKI Board of Management for permission to refer to papers prepared by the Institute, some of which have been published as articles in the journal *Ministry*. At one step removed I have also gained from being able to read and use material produced by the Alban Institute in the United States. My thanks also go to the past and present staff of, and the contributors to, *Action Information* and its successor *Congregations*. I have read and adapted contributions from their article-writers and tried to apply them to our European situation. In more recent years my colleagues at Avec provided great stimulation and a new discipline in ways of analysis and consultancy. I am grateful to be able to use some of the material we developed together in my own writings here.

My pen pictures of congregational life are not drawn from any one situation and certainly do not describe real characters. The situations I talk about have been recognized on both sides of the Atlantic and of the North Sea. They 'ring true' because congregations do seem to have some universal characters and characteristics. It is those I have tried to piece together in pictures which are entirely of my own construction.

Putting together a book about congregations, which will connect with many denominations, means that I have found difficulty in describing the titles and groups for each church. My decision has been to range from priest to minister to vicar to pastor in order to emphasize the universal nature of the characteristics I am describing. The same has been true for synods, boards, trustees, dioceses and districts. I hope that this will not prove too confusing but will make the point about a universality of experience.

My hope is that in exploring this very different organization, the congregation, with its multi-layered life and its particularity as a community of faith, something new and revealing will emerge and that the quest for richer understandings will go on.

MALCOLM GRUNDY
Pentecost 1998

Introduction

Why does anyone go to church? I used to ask myself this when I looked out over congregations in the early days of my ordained ministry. Then I decided that the question was better not asked. Who am I to wonder why anyone else is there? I pushed the idea to the back of my mind. For more than twenty-five years it became the great unapproachable question; but it never really went away. I found that occasional articles appeared with amusing pieces of analysis, but no one really took it head-on. Groups and consultations enjoyed the discussions I steered on the subject. Why *do* people go to church and, if they go once, why would they want to go back again?

I can no longer ignore this question. It has to be lifted from the recesses of my mind and explored in detail. All those occasional pieces of writing by other people need to be brought together. This will not be a 'church growth' book, nor only a textbook for students; it is for all those who 'go to church'. Mine will be an exploration of that hitherto unaskable question. Perhaps by the end, some of those who wonder why they keep on attending church will understand themselves a little more. Hopefully we shall have explored what is going on within the life of that unique group in society we call a congregation. We shall come to understand why some congregations fail and why others experience growth. It might become clear to each of us that our presence in a congregation will contribute to a particular stage in its life – whether of expansion, tension, complacency or decline.

Personal survival

My experiences in the places in which I have worked made me examine my own views and faith in ways I would never have imagined when I first sat at the back of the church as a member of our East Anglian village congregation. Many other things bear in on my own story, or any of our Christian stories. Our country has changed internally and in relation to other countries in the world. Permanent groups of unemployed people seem to have become a fact of life. No longer are Christians a majority of worshippers in some of our cities: other faiths have their own distinctive place in our country. Church decline has continued. The balance of denominations has shifted. The Church of England no longer has the majority – the Roman Catholic Church has that. Many new sects and Christian groups exist. Together, they outnumber either of the principal denominations. A more vigorous kind of evangelicalism has sprung up within many denominations. In common with sister churches around the world, Anglicans are getting used to having both men and women ordained to the priesthood. Those who have stayed in their denominations are, by their very presence, wrestling with the question of survival. They are also wondering how best to get any kind of sustenance from a congregation made up of people with such different histories and memories and who have such varying expectations of what they can get from 'going to church'.

Many more people have a great sympathy with churchgoing and a sincere, if unexpressed, set of personal beliefs. A wide range of such people will come to church for special events as well as for weddings, baptisms and funerals. While being very supportive and often willing to give money and do pieces of work for 'the church' they will not commit themselves to membership. 'Believing yet not belonging' has become almost a catchphrase to describe attitudes to churchgoing in many countries in the developed world. There is also quite a strong view that church attendance out of habit and through familiarity might produce attitudes of 'belonging without believing' if some members of congregations were pressed about exactly how they would express the faith they have.[1]

Different responses

What has also always intrigued me is when other people who have lived through the same period and who have had similar experiences come to quite different conclusions from me about what is happening in our churches. Even more strikingly, very little thought and research is being done to understand the life of our local churches. That is why I have called this book *Understanding Congregations*. It is easy for Anglicans in England to hide behind the idea of 'the parish' and not be over concerned about who is or who is not a member of the regular congregation. This is a luxury which is not available anywhere else in the Anglican Communion or to any other denomination. The study of the life of the congregation and the place of the minister within it is, I think, one of the most fundamental needs which face our churches at the moment. Hence my exploration in this book.

My own journey and story

I first went to church with both my parents in a small country village with a large building and a smallish congregation. I made friends with other churchgoing teenagers through the diocesan activities and first felt a call to ordination. After two years in a drawing office in Bedford I spent a year with Community Service Volunteers in Manchester. I lived in an inner-city vicarage and then in the front room of a terraced house and discovered how trapped many poor people were by their circumstances. The local church had been demolished and every Saturday evening we carried the church furnishings into the school hall for Sunday worship. I began my entry into clerical life by training at King's College, London. This was in the context of 'Swinging Sixties' London. Across the Strand from King's, students from the London School of Economics were protesting about student life and the way in which their college was governed. LSE students burst into King's with their noisy protests. What I remember most was an outraged Professor of Ecclesiastical History telling us how impossible all this protest was since the college was really only the academic staff. Students were there as some sort of convenient appendage. The contrast between radicalism and conservatism hit me strongly for the first time in these two settings.

Studies took the same course. We were the *Honest to God* generation. John Robinson's book had first of all been a shock to the orthodox believer. Then it emerged as the vehicle by which so many intelligent and inquiring people could say 'I'm not sure, but I want to stay with it and know more'. At King's we discovered in more detail what Tillich and Bonhoeffer really wrote. Of course, we took into ourselves the pieces which suited and only in later years came to understand the significance of such questions as Bonhoeffer's 'Who really is Jesus Christ for us today?' At that time few of us understood Teilhard de Chardin but Sidney Evans, our Dean, would not let us forget his significance to modern thinking. Biblical criticism was liberating as we were at first shocked and then relieved that so many of those difficult, not to say contradictory, biblical texts required intelligent and critical understanding but were not required as articles of faith. A 'communist' vicar called Alan Ecclestone came to preach.

I spent the summer of 1966 in Boston, Massachusetts, running an inner city summer camp. Harvey Cox, author of *The Secular City*, was living and working with a congregation just down the road. Evenings were spent in intense student dialogue with him and with radical Catholics. I knew that I wanted to continue with these questions when I went to a parish.

After a search which taught me everything and nothing about the deployment of clergy, I moved to Doncaster Parish Church in South Yorkshire. Here I discovered 'civic religion' and was involved in chaplaincies in the railway and coal mining industries. The most hard-bitten men, the wildest training operatives and the most senior managers were equally pleased to see me. They talked about beliefs, values and Christianity with an ease and interest I rarely encountered in church members. I was thrown back to look at Bonhoeffer's great questions of how we speak to people in their strength rather than creating and exploiting a sense of weakness.[2] What was he saying then and what was I experiencing now? These chaplaincies led on to full-time work with the Sheffield Industrial Mission and immersion in the issues of industries and people undergoing immense changes in their lives. Over a period of eleven years we had a procession of visitors to our houses from around the world and a series of students on courses from our own theological colleges. Questions about the relationship of church to society pressed hard on all of our thinking, as did the place of the parish and the congregation in Christian mission and in the formation and support of lay people.

Then I went to London, a city secular, pluralist, multi-faith and Christian all at the same time. As Director of Education and Community in one of the largest dioceses in the world, with the recruitment of a talented staff, we set about supporting the clergy and congregations, some of which were as real and some as unreal as any in the world. The forging of a policy for this work was exciting and felt like breaking new ground. It involved an analysis of the infrastructure of a diocese as well as the development of courses linked to an overall policy of training for clergy and laity. This experience has left an indelible mark on my thinking. I learned that structures needed to be understood and influenced if lasting change was to take place. Only different ways of understanding church and of strategic planning would encourage and allow Christian people to live and behave in ways appropriate for ministry in changed situations.

Life and leadership in a local congregation

By then it was the mid-1980s. I went to Huntingdon in Cambridgeshire to set up a team ministry. After all this mission, education and training work, to go to a parish where people actually said and did all those things I had been told about on our courses was sobering. It was like walking onto a film set. People actually did the things which course members had been describing and analysing with me for so many years! Some of the people were saints; others grew in ways none of us thought possible at first. Together we used the Adult Catechumenate as a way of bringing enquirers and believers to a deeper faith. It was fun and it was hard work. I became immersed in the culture of congregations – which is real life for all of a working life for most of our clergy. I experienced the static and the dynamic nature of congregations as they learned to live with their clergy and as their 'life cycle' began an upward rise after years of relative decline. I learned ecumenism on the ground by working with our local Methodist Church. We all felt the significance of the change of our title from Council of Churches to Churches Together.

The Edward King Institute for Ministry Development was begun in 1986, the same year that I went to Huntingdon. Since I knew its founders, Christopher Laurence and Norman Todd, I was in at the start and was the founder and first editor of its journal *Ministry*. This has meant that I have had a steady stream of articles and books about congregations flowing across my desk for more than a decade. It has also been an eye-opener to see what organizations such as the Alban Institute in the United States are offering in resources for parishes. Material from Australia and New Zealand has come with refreshing insights. The experience of many years of work with the church in Sweden, which came through running courses in the Diocese of Växjö and elsewhere, has allowed me to test out some of these ideas with friends and colleagues in a church very similar to ours in England.

Recent developments for me have included three years working in Britain and Ireland with Avec, a consultancy agency for church and community, and my present job as Archdeacon of Craven in the Diocese of Bradford. In both of these situations I have had to learn the skills of consultancy and practise ways of reconciling congregations and voluntary organizations when there have been internal disputes. I have also worked as consultant to the Anglican Society of St Francis and for the lay members of the Franciscan Third Order. It has also been a great insight into another denomination to be able to work with a number of Roman Catholic religious orders. In 1994 a group of us set up a new networking organization, MODEM: Managerial and Organisational Disciplines for the Enhancement of Ministry. This has brought together a vibrant group of those who are concerned to exchange good management practice in secular and church organizations.

This autobiographical way into what I want to write about congregations is important for me because I am convinced that each of us needs to know where the other is coming from if there is to be understanding, reconciliation and growth. Journey, story and assumptions are important elements in our understanding of how organizations work and for our glimpses of the faith of others. They are essential to the understanding of how adults learn. I believe that the same process is integral to the understanding of congregations.

Such a review is not a self-indulgent piece of biography. It describes a panorama of events which has been the raw material for reflection on change. In setting down my own views in the following chapters I am aware of how much I have been helped by many others who wanted to make the same enquiries. Some have since decided to leave the church, others are in the same local situations and have experienced change without moving; others now have to help to manage and lead our denominations or churches in other countries. What is common to all those in these networks is that we want to be able to stand back and ask what is happening around us. In the Edward King Institute we call this *reflective practice*. I hope that as I unfold the many ideas which we have shared together, friends and colleagues will recognize the discussion and their contribution in it. Words spoken and exciting seminars shared can all too often seem like footprints in the sand, washed away with the passage of time and by the pressure of everyday events. In re-assembling contributions and articles with a focus on the life of the local congregation, I hope that many more will be able to share in the debate and that our local churches can understand how to adapt, change and grow.

Notes

1   See the chapter by Grace Davie, 'Christian belief in modern Britain: the tradition becomes vicarious' in *New Soundings* (Darton, Longman and Todd, 1997).
2   This question has been explored most recently by Peter Selby in *Grace and Mortgage* (Darton, Longman and Todd, 1997).

1

Understanding Churchgoing

Most active Christian people need to go to church. Where those needs come from and how they are met is worth a systematic exploration. Some people still go through habit. Others go, again and again, in the hope that they will find something special which will change their lives. Many people who persist in their churchgoing know that they do get something special but they cannot put it into words. Some of the same people express tremendous frustration at what they experience in church. They want better music, more for children, a liturgy in which more people participate – and continuous review and revision. Others, usually in the same congregation, are fighting to preserve a tradition and to prevent the erosion of what they regard as sacred as well as familiar. Clergy, who were once 'lay' members of a congregation themselves, attempt to hold these fragile coalitions together and pray that they can retain their integrity on the way.

The first Christians, meeting in small groups, often in secret, were as much aware of the need for survival as for spiritual nurture and growth. They did not meet in public buildings with centuries of tradition. They met in private in one another's homes or in secret rooms. From the very vivid memory of the Last Supper, and the need to pray together, meetings of Christians took on a recognizable shape. Services, as we now call them, were constructed. A ritual emerged which was similar if not common to all the groups. When greater religious freedom emerged, buildings were constructed and people made daily and weekly visits to them to rehearse these liturgies, to support one another and to initiate new members.

It is a considerable step from what went on in those early groups of Christians to what happens in many of our churches today. Nevertheless, there is a continuous thread and some of the very same words are used. Congregations which might be called 'alive' certainly have an atmosphere which in our imaginations we may think was something like that in places where the first Christians met. In many other churches people attend through a sense of obligation. The atmosphere there is more that of survival in a changing world and church than that of the need to provide a ready and open welcome to newcomers, or even to those churchgoers who have moved into their community.

Traditions and 'The Tradition'

One of the most intractable difficulties in discussing almost anything about church life is an inability to distinguish between traditions and the Christian tradition. Arguments frequently flare up over the changing of a tradition within a congregation which may have only existed for a relatively few years. There is an emotional need for many to defend a tradition which is really no other than a familiarity with churchgoing from a happier time, whether it be with the youth club, a young family or a particular group of friends. Liturgical traditionalists of a High Church kind are nostalgic in defending a Victorian or Edwardian re-clothing of medieval rituals. Traditionalist Evangelicals will be even more aware that evangelicalism today bears little or no resemblance to the Low Church worship characteristic for most of this century. Perhaps where most might agree without knowing is that in these 'post-modern' days they have an ever-lessening adherence of the tradition of their denomination. Even though we have been shaped by denominational roots, allegiances now cross over relatively easily and common ground is found beyond the ecclesiological divide with those who think in a similar way, be it charismatic or liberal or conservative.

Where there appears to be less of a debate within the churches is in the willing rediscovery of 'The Tradition' which is common ground for us all. We know of the tradition which St Paul said he received and which he was passing on. We know, through his letters, what a faith he built from that tradition. It is that Christ lived, died and rose again for the forgiveness of our sins so that we might share in his new life. We gain peace with God through faith alone and not by any works of our own. The church mediates this faith by its teachings and through its sacraments. This is where searchers want to be. It is in the connections with this God-given relationship, passed on through our faith traditions, that those on a new-found faith exploration find a resonance and no little excitement.

Change or decay?

Change faces all those who go to church. If everything else might be ignored, it costs more money now to go to church. No longer do investments from the past or rich patrons cushion churches and congregations. Now, active church members have to dip deeply into their pockets to pay for the maintenance of their buildings and for the support of their clergy; most prefer to give in that order of priority.

There are now far fewer clergy available. Some congregations are fortunate and have 'their own' minister. In these situations it is possible to maintain a traditional set of expectations and to have the clergy at the centre of many of the activities in the local church. With an able minister and supportive lay people, churches of this type can flourish. They appear to work best in small towns or in the suburbs of cities. In a phrase from Ted Wickham, a pioneer of industrial mission in England, does God seem to have a preference for such areas?

Over recent years more and more congregations have 'shared' a minister. Sometimes, with great effort, expectations have been met. In many other places God appears to be showing a different kind of preference by leading laity and ministers to experiment with new patterns of 'local' ministry. Here an impossible situation has been turned into an opportunity and new patterns of organization for the life of the local church are emerging. With them come a new and revitalized spirituality. Lay people see more clearly the place which they have in the life of the local church and in the communities where they live and where they work. It is they, as well as the clergy, who are called to what is now known as 'ministry' when they live out in a more shared way the implications of what it means to be a Christian. New life has risen from what looked like the death of an established order. The significance of this for Christians is a statement in itself.

Many clergy have had to come to terms with a way of life which was not what they expected in the early years after their ordination. In some cases they are expected to have a pattern of work for which they were not trained. Later I shall explore 'models' or pictures of clerical life which sustain many people. Here we need to recognize that there has had to be tremendous revision of an age-old view of the clergy. Ministers today, if they are to survive and to avoid 'burn-out', have to pace themselves differently. A valuing or re-valuing of the essential role of clergy has gone on. Many of their peripheral tasks have been made redundant or are now done by congregation members in their spare time.

There has been a certain amount of drift or pragmatism in the way in which advantage has been taken of these changes. I want to explore in some detail in the chapter 'Understanding Collaborative Ministry' just what 'sharing out the vicar's jobs' has come to look like. There is in many congregational discussions a rather loose use of terms like 'shared' and 'collaborative' to embrace these changes. One of my local farmers calls it 'paying more for less'. In many places the ending of the old style, where congregational life rises and falls according to the ability and the interests of the minister, has been a liberation. God is doing new things here and we need to wait, listen and take stock. Once it was the clergy who saw themselves as prophets, priests and pastors. Now we know again that this is the calling of all the baptized. It is a sobering and an exciting rediscovery.

Starting from the other end

Let me begin with a very radical assumption, that the way in which we set out our church organization at the moment is simply the wrong way round. What we have is the deposit of history. To be effective as Christian people today, and to be able to bring others to faith, we need different methods and structures. Could the system of local congregations each with their clergy resident or close by be an anachronism held over from an age now past? Congregations with a life and vitality of their own need different structures. To influence a nation, churches need to operate in quite different ways. If we begin by looking at congregations from the other end of the tunnel we will see them differently and perhaps understand what we should keep and what will have to wither away and die.

I have been unable to escape from this perspective and from these questions since I began researching into the thinking behind industrial mission.[1] The Abbé Godin was a person who attempted to push his church and its ministry forward with dramatic new strategies and action in the France of the 1930s and 1940s. In *France Pagan?* he sets out the missionary task as he sees it for the Catholic Church in the France of his time. The chapter 'Missionary methods' describes a meeting with a mission priest from Central Africa and a priest in Paris. The two have a dialogue about their respective missionary methods in an urban, sprawling city and in a country with very sparse resources.

> 'You people simply don't know what a mission is. . . . According to what you say you have no more regular church-goers than we have – and our Christians are of a different kind. We have about one tenth the number of your priests . . . Our pecuniary resources can't compete with those of the capital or of our great towns . . . and yet Christ's Kingdom is growing.
>
> And if we multiplied our priests by ten, if we had an impressive bank roll, if we employed your methods, our results would be the same as yours. The ground we had won would be maintained with difficulty; bit by bit we should retreat *as you are doing.*'[2]

The dialogue between the two men continued with the berating of the Catholic Church in France for admitting children to baptism without a real desire from the parents to bring the children up as Christians, marriages of all who ask, burial without the last rites and much more. Here for me were the strong echoes of all that Bonhoeffer was saying about 'cheap grace' in the first chapter of *The Cost of Discipleship* where those in his own church were chastized for offering forgiveness without repentance, baptism without church discipline, and communion without personal confession.[3]

The mission priest went on to tell Godin about the catechumenate and long preparation before baptism and communion. People took risks to their family ties and for their lives when they left their tribal customs to become Christians. Just the same has been said by many who have returned from the mission field and who came to us at Avec. Their experiences from different cultures have hardly been heard.

The significant remark for the context of our congregation studies is here:

> The missionary concluded to Godin quietly: 'The great difference is this, you are assuming the existence of a Christian community which has in fact disappeared. You help crowds of people perform acts designed to bring them to God individually. But nothing follows. You forget, too, that brilliant statistics are less important than the inner values of a Christian community. Thus you lose a great deal of time and employ many men without a result.'

That is what I mean when I suggest that we might begin to look at our situation from the other end. We need to ask what structures and resources we need to help us get to where we want to be. Is it fruitless to continue to pour time and money into a structure of church life which is largely unproductive? How can local and shared ministry schemes make a difference? What does it mean to try to take the members of a local congregation seriously?

In my own time, work with the Church of Sweden bears out the need for such questions. Supported by the church tax, local congregations have almost all the resources they need, yet church attendance is stunningly low. Could this be because the real questions about the structure of a missionary congregation have never had to be asked? Only now when the threat of the removal of this tax is looming have churches woken up to the urgent need for analysis, training and restructuring. Some exciting and innovative programmes for welcoming newcomers have been developing which follow the methods of the Adult Catechumenate. Many in the Scandinavian churches have found it tremendously difficult to accept the ordination of women. Here, as in other denominations, the question of how a church changes while still being faithful to its roots and tradition has been a painful and a formative experience. With their different histories such questions have an importance and an urgency in the churches right across Europe.

An English priest who tried to look at this situation in his parish retired in the year I was ordained. Alan Ecclestone was Vicar of Darnall in Sheffield from 1942 to 1969. In his retirement he reflected on the experiences of an exceptional Christian life and wrote about his efforts and the sources from which his missionary methods sprang. In *A Staircase for Silence* he used as a basis the work and writings of Charles Péguy, a Frenchman searching for spiritual depth through writing and verse who was active in the early years of this century.

Péguy was severely critical of the parish system in France and of the curés who, he felt, had lost their congregations because they had imposed a dead language upon their people, excluding from the sphere of religious devotion those things which were the realities of their working lives. Ecclestone concludes:

> The outcome in terms of the spiritual life had been a disaster for both. A dumb laity made for an arrogant inwardly-fearful clergy, for a hollowness where communion should have reigned . . . We are charged, as though by chance, with making people communicate through us who do not want to communicate to them.[4]

The congregation which Ecclestone established in Darnall was one which was way ahead of its time. It had a weekly parish meeting to discuss anything and everything. There was advanced liturgy with an altar brought forward, but most of all, the lay people had a central place in the discussion of everything which took place in their parish. Ecclestone wrote in a visionary way about what a congregation should be and I shall begin the chapter on 'Understanding Survival' with his basic and, for me, tremendously influential piece of writing.[5]

Below the surface in a congregation

We also have to address the question of the relationship of a congregation to its surrounding community. This, too, is a fundamental and controversial missionary question for our churches today. In my Archdeacon's Visitation questions for 1995 I asked clergy and churchwardens in towns and villages in my parts of Yorkshire, Lancashire and Cumbria for their opinions about the relationship of the church to the community in which it is set. What I received back showed a clear division of opinion. There were a minority, both urban and rural, who saw the population of a parish in virtually the same way as they understood their local congregation. There is a great sense of history in this and it gives a particular understanding about the relationship of the parish church to its local population. Some of those who saw their situation in this way found it difficult to respond to questions about mission and drawing people into a describable, week by week, congregation where membership is identified and commitment in faith, time and money is expected.

Others who gave answers, again in both urban and rural situations, were able to speak about a ministry aimed at drawing people into a deeper faith by association with the weekly or monthly worshipping congregation. Those giving answers from this perspective were able to think in terms of programmes, targets and measurable achievement.

There has been a dialogue between church people in England for more than fifty years about how to confront those who either have a tenuous relationship with a church or who only use it when they require a rite of passage to be performed. Edward Bailey[6] has done much to stimulate this discussion about 'folk religion', or 'implicit religion' as it is now called. With some distinguished sociologists of religion he has helped many of us to explore what the deep layers of religion in any community really look like. Only some of these layers are Christian.

'Pay as you go'

It is now very apparent that any church which has to pay for its own livelihood, as now does even the Church of England, will have to identify its membership and ask them to contribute a reasonable, regular sum to the maintenance of that denomination. This is nothing new to all the other denominations who have had to maintain their own livelihood from their very origins, albeit helped by wealthy industrialists or patrons. This defining of identity has also had its manifestations in the emergence of a much more overt faith. We are asked – required – to decide how we want to express what faith we have. If what we want is there in our local church we pay to sit happily with it. If it is not there, we shop around, travel, and pay for what we want somewhere else. All this puts a great strain on the concept of the local parish church providing 'something for everyone' worship. Take-it-or-leave-it congregations in local communities find they have given themselves a life-threatening illness.

To those outside the regular worshipping congregation this is all very strange. Local people have been led to believe that the church will always be there for them. Unfortunately those same people come with an expectation that the worship and the life of the congregation will be much the same as when they visited the church for a service the last time, and that it will cost just about as much! A test of faith and classes before a baptism come as quite a shock. A funeral service with strange new words is disturbing, as is the revelation that families cannot have just what they want on a tombstone!

Have we changed or have they? What *has* changed is the relationship of a congregation to its neighbourhood. Folk religion may be dressed up with a new name but the questions it poses about ritual and behaviour are very serious indeed. David Martin, a writer about the sociology of religion, has said that those who come for baptisms, marriages and funerals are looking for a 'Sacred Arch' through which to pass at times of significant transition in their lives. This is borne out by a number of studies of ritual and ceremony surrounding rites of passage in the former Soviet Union.[7] Very many want to mark important events in their lives with some kind of ritual. Where we see Christian things they see faith, if at all, through a glass very darkly. In our congregations and through our clergy we are doing something for and with those occasional or non-churchgoers in our communities.

How these changes affect life in the local congregation

Amid all this search for new understandings of what congregational life is about there is inevitably a large degree of uncertainty. People react to such changing circumstances in many different ways. There has certainly been a trend, which is mirrored in the rest of English society, to move towards more cautious positions in order to defend what security remains. Within the denominations this has meant a retreat from outreach and the work of specialist ministries towards retrenchment and the placing of resources into congregational life. The consequence of this atmosphere for those who prefer an innovative stance when change has been in the air has been for many clergy and laity to choose to sit more lightly to their denominations and to their local congregations. It has meant, as Christopher

Laurence has pointed out in *Ministry*,[8] that a number of talented clergy with professionally developed specialisms have decided to become self-employed consultants working on contracts for churches, voluntary organizations, health authorities and commercial companies.

It has been the experience of many in industry and commerce that the first tell-tale sign of terminal decline is the closure of the Research and Development department. The investment has been cut, to make a short-term saving, in the place where the thinking about products and experiment through projects is taking place. Consequently, companies can only continue producing the same goods until they become obsolete or are overtaken by what a competitor has to offer. Comparisons are sometimes dangerous and inappropriate, but churches which do not encourage experiment and innovation may well find themselves overtaken by a similar series of events.

Management and leadership

One of the key questions to be unveiled as this exploration develops is about how leadership is to be understood in relation to these substantial changes which are taking place within the denominations. It is the task of a leader today to shape and mould opinion and to give direction to the work of others. More often than not, this is done through vision and example rather than by coercion and sanction.[9]

Church management has become a popular, if controversial, concept as organizational studies have been applied to the local congregations. One of the new groupings looking at this is MODEM – Managerial and Organisational Disciplines for the Enhancement of Ministry. In their book called *Management and Ministry* a range of contributors have tried to bring such thinking into the mainstream of church life.[10] Their series of seminars across England might begin to frame something of a staff college for in-service training within the denominations.

Thomas J. Sweetser SJ, writing in the journal *Human Development*, has made an interesting distinction between management and leadership.[11] To illustrate the difference, he chose the situation of a parish in the United States which was deciding to re-locate its school. The first example of response was for the minister to call together a group of financial and building specialists to come up with a solution to the problem. Once they were agreed and the plans made, then the minister and the group had the task of persuading the congregation to accept the plan and raise the money. That, Sweetser says, is a good example of management.

For leadership to be seen he describes the same situation in a different way. This time he describes the minister as a person gifted with intuition and insight. He calls together the congregation and asks them to produce their own creative solutions. They reject the most logical solution about the replacement of the school and come up with exciting new ideas about a youth and social centre incorporated into the renovation of the existing building. They saw what the real local needs of the church and the community were at that time and proposed a solution which would spring the congregation into the future. This Sweetser describes as leadership. The parishioners, after detailed consultation and costing, could say 'We as a parish are being called to do this by the Spirit'. They were not being managed to accept other people's solutions to a problem which reflected a past need of that congregation. I call this 'looking at the problem from the other end'.

In a congregation both management and leadership are necessary. Management keeps a parish functioning well and running smoothly. Without good management the hymns do not get chosen, the hall is badly let, the finances get in a mess and very much more. The services which a congregation is expected to deliver to the community would be lacking. People would be frustrated, members of the congregation desert and the downward spiral begins. Surprisingly, to the unenlightened, a congregation can get along better without good leadership than it can without good management. Congregations are maintained through management; they are changed by leadership.

Traditionalists will say that there is a well-tried formula for an effective minister in a parish. It is preach, teach, visit. I would not disagree with that. The difference here is that we shall be exploring what preaching, teaching and visiting might mean for today and who should be doing what. We shall look at the new relationship already forced into existence between clergy and laity. It may become clearer who should expect what from whom, what the priest or minister should do, what should be shared – and what sharing means. There is always the easy-to-avoid question of what might need to be ended.

When we look at what congregations are and what they are for, we can begin to gain some idea of how effective they are in their aims and in their work. Some ideas shared will lead to more efficient management, others perhaps to inspired leadership. We all learn by reacting, questioning, being challenged or by being affirmed in whatever it is we are being called to as we share in that priesthood and discipleship which is the joy of all God's people.

The excitement of staying in

Congregations are models, examples of what life together in community can be like. It is that hopefulness which makes people come back, even after a bad experience. Within the congregational or community life of 20 or 200 people many basic human experiences are shared. Here people have a place where they can celebrate together and where they can grieve together. They also learn how to celebrate and grieve for others. They, we, learn how to tolerate, to forgive and be forgiven. All learn how to live with differences.

Within all this is an experience of God which is both corporate and communal and also personal and private. It is not a static experience or one which feeds only on past memories. The idea of a congregation as a model of community arises from a concept of faith which is both dynamic and forward-looking. It is something of a village example of community which many hope to see in their broader lives, but do not.

Congregations who begin to get it right cannot be inward-looking. Those who catch a glimpse of what is going on become drawn into an infectious atmosphere whose life-blood is the events and drama of the world. In such congregations believers and seekers can start from the other end with their hopes and dreams, and test out what practical Christian living is all about – and what they need from their local church!

Congregations and worship

At the beginning of my discussions about this book I had a very interesting conversation with a publisher's editor. He responded to my ideas by saying that the concept of 'a congregation' was not one held by most people who went to church. The idea of a congregation is one which clergy or church leaders have when they 'look down the nave'. People say they are a member of such-and-such a church, but not of its congregation. He may be right but many years of giving talks to all kinds of people in many countries suggests to me that things might be a little different.

He was certainly right in that many people have not, through the centuries, gone to church 'to join a congregation'. It seems to me that things are different today. This is my experience – not least in the recitations I hear of the many reasons why people do not go to church. More often than not they give me reasons about the friendliness – or lack of it – experienced by them from other churchgoers or from ministers!

Where that editor was absolutely right is that it would be wrong to think that churchgoing was only a matter of wanting to meet other people and share in a friendly atmosphere. People go into church buildings and engage with our liturgies more than anything else to feel something about God. Many cannot find the words to express that search but the lines from 'Amazing Grace' get it right in a popular way for many people:

I once was lost but now am found,
was blind but now I see.

Church buildings and God

The visit to a church building is a strange and yet comforting experience. For the vast majority of people in the developed world, entry into a church is something strange and unusual. Sharing in a service is even more alien. Those who go regularly are very aware of this when they encounter the visitor who has crept in on a quiet weekday or the many who come only for weddings or baptisms. Yet something is experienced by very many people, and some of them come back. When I was an industrial chaplain I was continually amazed at the stories people in the factories told me about the lovely churches they visited when they were on holiday. I could never quite bring myself to suggest they gave themselves a treat and went occasionally now that they were home. Working in the delightful Yorkshire Dales as I do now, I am very aware that visitors return with a great regularity to the same holiday church, some several times a year. This building many miles away from home and interfering friends and neighbours is 'their church'. People do find something of the God they are seeking in the atmosphere of the building, its beauty, simplicity or tranquillity. They also respond, in their own ways, to the welcome they are given.

Such sentiments were tested out by the surprising public response to the death of Princess Diana, when many thousands of people went into church buildings, lit candles, placed flowers and signed books of condolence. The cynics, who for years had said how strange it was for many people to enter a church building, were confounded. The throwing of flowers before her coffin on its way to burial was almost medieval in its enactment. Much re-assessing is still going on as a result of this spontaneous outburst of public sentiment. It is clear that, as well as mourning an attractive public figure who did much good, deep personal feelings and hurts were being released in public and private displays of mourning. Religious observance paid a part in this and Christian buildings and symbols tried to play their part.

Churchgoing and familiarity

Entering a church is also about memories from the past. The smells are about childhood and Sunday School in otherwise long-forgotten days belonging to another world. Some church buildings are about memories of parents, baptisms, and of friends. All of this is right and can be built upon – but only by church attenders and in their own ways. No one can or should be made to go to church. Willing attendance touches something deep within a person; forced attendance brings resistance and sometimes revulsion. Familiarity and something deep touched is about an understanding of spirituality. The journey or search for security and meaning has taken another step. The kind of welcome which develops a sometimes right and sometimes nostalgic familiarity helps strangers to feel able to return. Enthusiasm encourages some and repels others. It is a certain characteristic of churchgoing today that a service which is easy to get into and where words are easy to pick up will attract newcomers – but they do not stay unless there is something more below the surface which takes them on. Preaching is also important. This can be a place where the Christian story is told afresh to those who do not know it. For the first time in centuries in the West the Christian Gospel is news – good news – to whole generations of people.

Bishop Michael Adie has put this very well in his first book, *Held Together: An Experiment in Coherence,* written just after his retirement:

> The treason of the cleric is to trivialize the gospel and package God in easily available quantities, with the result that we lose the mystery and wonder. As any worthy minister ascends the pulpit steps he is trembling: how can he in the few minutes now available to him convey the wonder and mystery of God in modern terms? How can his pint-pot mind contain all the water that flows from the fountain of life?[12]

The balance between searching and certainty is a difficult one to strike, as is that between emotionalism and attempts at rational logic. What we all know is that when it works and comes together an infectious atmosphere exists and a special time has come in a church building with a group of trusting, loving people – they have become a congregation!

A sacramental deepening

Going to church can be an individual thing. Ironically, many people say that it is when they receive the sacrament of Holy Communion that they most want to feel alone with God. The continuation of the early morning service or the quiet evening communion is a proof of this. A valuing of the sacraments is something which comes as the Christian life develops. In a very real way it is about drawing close to God through communion with others and by using the things of the earth – water, wine and bread – as vehicles to transcend mere human experience. Emil Brunner, the Lutheran theologian and a professor at Zurich University in the 1930s, wrote tellingly of the connection between understanding congregations and understanding the sacraments:

> The fellowship of faith is, however, an integral part of faith. It is possible to enjoy a work of art, a concert or a lecture, and be edified by it without the presence of any other person . . . *One cannot have faith alone.* Indeed the aim of the Word of God is to conquer this solitude by

leading us out of our isolation into fellowship with one
another. God's word and fellowship are inseparable.
Therefore our Lord instituted the sacraments that we
might not make a private concern of His word . . . God
did not create us to get along by ourselves, but that we
'should bear one another's burdens' . . . The sacraments
are the buttresses which keep the Church from falling
asunder because they do not permit a man to receive the
salvation of God alone. Only in the congregation, only in
confessing 'I need the other man' shall you receive God's
salvation. Otherwise you remain self-contained – and
unsaved.[13]

In willing participation as part of the life of a congregation,
which is a human–divine community, we learn to give and to
receive, to take and to share. In doing this we discover the God
who is among us in other people and in the familiar and the difficult things of this world.

Stated in a much less religious way, many churches are being
challenged to examine their internal life and their aims. Some –
many – will never have thought about these questions in relation
to church ever before. Even if such exercises are a full part of
working life, there is a great desire to 'leave all this behind when
we come to church'.

In the Diocese of Ripon and in a parish in Nottingham,
'Investors in People' has become a method of internal examination which might launch us into our necessarily more practical
further thinking about congregations and our place in them.[14]
The General Synod of the Church of England has also made a
study of how the concepts of Investors might be used to
encourage different ways of thinking in an organization. The
attractiveness of Investors in People is that it builds upon work
which is already being done in companies and now with schools
and charities. It emphasizes the involvement of everyone in setting goals together, it encourages the provision of good learning
opportunities and puts in place open methods for monitoring
and review as groups of people within an organization continue
to work together. This way of evaluation, originally designed for
industry, is finding appropriate adaptation and may well find a
different home in helping churches to understand their systems
and methods of communication.

The Investors in People Cycle

1. There should be a clear sense of purpose understood by everyone.
2. The contribution everyone can make to achieve that purpose should be indentified.
3. Everyone should be given the training and support they need to be able to make their contribution.
4. Everyone should evaluate how they are using their talents and resources so that the overall purpose can be achieved.

These principles form a cycle:

What are we trying to achieve? (Purpose)
What contribution can everyone make? (Planning)
What training and support are needed? (Implementation)
How well are we doing? (Evaluation)

Notes

1 Malcolm Grundy, *An Unholy Conspiracy* (Canterbury Press, 1993).

2 *France Pagan: The Mission of Abbé Godin*, trans. Maisie Ward (Catholic Book Club, 1949), p. 126.

3 D. Bonhoeffer, *The Cost of Discipleship* (SCM, 1964), p. 35.

4 Alan Ecclestone, *A Staircase for Silence* (Darton, Longman and Todd, 1977), p. 80.

5 Tim Gorringe, *Alan Ecclestone: Priest as Revolutionary* (Sheffield: Cairns Publications, 1994).

6 Edward Bailey, The Network for Implicit Religion, The Rectory, 58 High Street, Winterbourne, Bristol BS17 1JQ.

7 Christel Lane, 'Ritual and ceremony in contemporary Soviet society', *The Sociological Review* (May 1979), p. 253.

8 Christopher Laurence, 'Ministry: inside or outside?', *Ministry* (edition 19, Spring 1993).

9 See the chapter on 'Transforming leadership' in G. Arbuckle, *Refounding the Church* (Geoffrey Chapman, 1993).

10 John Nelson (ed.), *Management and Ministry* (Canterbury Press, 1996).

11 Thomas J. Sweetser SJ, 'Parish leadership versus parish management', *Human Development* (Autumn 1992); reprinted as Avec Occasional Paper no. 4.

12 Michael Adie, *Held Together: An Experiment in Coherence* (Darton, Longman and Todd, 1997), p. 61.

13 Emil Brunner, *Our Faith* (SCM, 1936, 1962), pp. 105–6.

14 Investors in People, Diocese of Ripon, c/o Julian Cummins, Beech House, Troy Road, Horsforth, Leeds LS18 5UW.

2

Understanding Survival

Where is your home congregation? Surprisingly, many people will not answer with the name of their present congregation. Home, in church terms, can mean a variety of things. Many now-lapsed people will be quite sure that if they belong anywhere, they are still members of the church in which they grew up. Others will refer back to the place where they were married or where they were when their children grew up. Even though people have moved on and may attend a new church, sometimes even a different denomination, they will refer to their home church as the one, somewhere, which gave them something special. They will be aware of connecting a sense of place with particular religious experiences which evoke both a sense of reality in belief and a sense of rootedness which has never been cut off.

Many will be familiar with the situation of two or more congregations being merged. Occasionally, if the new congregation has a new name and a new church dedication then there will be a new sense of belonging. More often, when one congregation has 'won' and the others have 'lost', even though the church will be called St Mary's-with-St Mark's-with-St John's, old allegiances survive. When asked, congregation members all too often will say they still belong to the old St Mark's or St John's. Even worse is the smugness of the congregation which thinks it has got the message and the family-feeling right. A little like the Pharisee against the Tax Collector (Luke 18.9–14), many people thank God that they worship in 'their own' church and that they are not like those poor people down the road who have to put up with – whatever it is – but, however inexplicably, seem to like it![1]

Congregations are all different. Some will differ in warmth, some in atmosphere created either by the building or by the people in it. Some will have the 'feel' of them affected beyond all else by the liturgies, formal or informal, which they choose to use. The person taking a service will have his or her own special effect, as will the level of congregational participation. All congregations are either growing or declining. A special characteristic of a congregation is its particular resilience both to changing and to ending its life. Rather than face conflict, many congregations choose to keep unresolved differences below the surface. This can be a strength as well as a weakness. At best this shows how a faith community has learned to live with difference, at worst it reflects an unwillingness to face questions and problems which are contributing to its demise.

A congregation to survive in?

Alan Ecclestone, in a passage about what a congregation might be like, has set a benchmark for me. He begins not with statistical or social analysis or with exclusive divisions about churchmanship or ecclesiology but with an inclusive vision of people living together in community. In *A Staircase for Silence* he talked about a congregation being a body of people drawn and held together in a spirit that prompts the members to care for, respect and love each other. He saw it as the embodiment in any place of what he called the 'I-in-you, you-in-me' relationship which Christ prayed for. A people-sized congregation, he said, would be small enough to permit true understanding to grow up between its members and one in which each person's life would be extended by the confrontation of diversities, character and achievements of the other members. Each person is encouraged to be themselves but to relate to a common life which is enriched by that which each supplies and becomes more than the sum of their gifts.

He wrote of the frustration of many church members:

Scattered among the people in our fragmented churches today there are those who hunger for something other than what they see, who are in pain because the church they belong to seems hopelessly stuck fast in a way of life that by no stretch of imagination can be described in terms of leaven or salt or light, who realise daily that the words used to speak of the church are far from being embodied in it. They know that the fellowship talked of does not take hold in a workmanlike way of the intricate fabric of human affairs nor confront the world in any decisive fashion.[2]

Could this be a paragraph which finds a resonance around the world? If so then Ecclestone, in almost prophetic form, frames an idea with 'Let us suppose then', and goes on to paint a picture of clergy and laity starting from the other end. Not with a view of reforming what we have but of meeting to ask one another what a parish seeking for this kind of future might do. What would it be like for people who had been in the same congregation for years to find a way of opening up their hearts to one another and thus making communication possible not only between one another but between themselves and God? Referring to the Papal Encyclical *Ecclesiam Suam* he describes prayer as dialogue, as part of the dialogue of salvation, begun by God with 'his' people. In a wonderfully contrasting statement he remarks, following the affirmation of sentiments which go with that Encyclical, 'An eternal foundation does not exclude the need to begin anew'. Unless there is something of that willingness to begin anew within every congregation, the path towards decline is already being walked. The re-establishment of the concept of a holy and God-centred congregation does not begin with programmes for renewal; it begins with waiting, with listening, with dialogue in prayer. We are not looking for the next miracle worker or the next analysis which will help us to take a tiny step forward. We are nurturing an idea; we are looking at the situation from a different perspective. We are listening to what those outside are asking for and we are waiting on God for new patterns to emerge.

The Merlin principle

A fascinating way of describing this seeing things from a different perspective, even from the other end, has been used by Charles Smith in an article called 'Leadership and strategic intent: the Merlin factor'.[3] He says that the principal impediment to changing an organization's strategic direction is its existing culture. Change is limited by people's current beliefs about what is possible. In his interviews with 'visionary' people and innovators he concluded that changing people's beliefs about the future can produce extraordinary improvements in their performance. He calls this the 'Merlin factor' after the legendary magician who was able to construct the present because he came from the future and lived backwards in time. Instead of beginning with an analysis of current or projected conditions in a company, Smith says, visionaries and innovators rely on a commitment to the future which could not be reasonably extrapolated from the state of the business at the time that commitment was made. They inspire others with a vision or dream of the future far beyond what the current scene might suggest.

We often speak of such people saying that 'they lived ahead of their time'. A church built on the hope of the resurrection with a clear belief that Christ has gone before us and that glimpses of the Kingdom are to be created or discovered here on earth will have these same forward-looking characteristics if it is going to change and survive. Churches, like many other organizations, have often re-created themselves in ways that far exceeded predictions of their possibilities.

Down from the mountain

Most of us have no choice but to begin with the congregation we have. There is no anecdotal Irishman to suggest it might be better if we started somewhere else. It is with *these* people in *this* building that we know God has placed us. What sort of a community is it? Could community be the wrong word? How do we know if it is home for us or not?

Who has looked at congregations and local churches and said anything which can be of help? In a book called *The Parish Church* edited by Giles Ecclestone, Alan's son, a group of writers associated with the Grubb Institute have set out a way of looking at attitudes portrayed by very different congregations.[4] In a rather polarized, but very formative way, they described and then debated what they called Communal Churches and what they called Associational Churches. We may well learn to 'know ourselves' by a brief look at the analysis which they gave.

Local communities expect things from their churches. What these things are frequently go unexpressed until something goes wrong or there is a clash of expectations of some kind. Building on these ideas the 'Grubb group' began by suggesting that any community defines itself by the boundaries it makes. How is it decided who is in and who is out? Can anyone come in and join? Is it easy to leave? Who says you can come in or you can leave? In a similar way these characteristics are becoming quite marked in the way congregations define themselves, in how they choose to relate to their surrounding communities. In my own way I have tried to put together the substance of what they were saying in the next two sections.

Two contrasting types of congregation

Communal congregations have certain characteristics (see Figure 2.1). In many ways they function as the parish church for their area, no matter what their denomination. The basic attitude is one of a responsibility for the well-being of all in the community. This responsibility is an idea in the mind more than anything else. It is shared by a majority of the members of the congregation. A number of factors of relatedness spring from this approach:

- People want to come to this church for baptisms, weddings and funerals.
- People in the community regard this church as 'theirs' whether they attend or not.
- Clergy feel it right to try to visit all in the parish. It is expected that they should.
- The purpose of the activities and teaching in the congregation is to equip people for service in the world.
- Events and happenings in the outside world are brought into the liturgies.
- Non-regulars complain when the services are changed.
- Clergy can handle living at this interface, they can cope with being treated in different roles according to where they are. They know they have a distinctive community-figure role.
- The major concern of the church is to show that it cares for the world.
- The congregation can tolerate differences within.

The communal congregation can also understand its relationship to the wider denomination in positive and organic ways.

- The diocese or district has the potential to become a living organism.

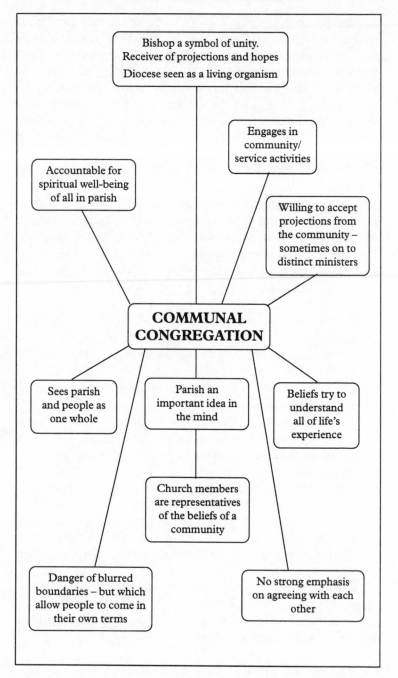

Figure 2.1 Communal congregations

- The deanery and diocese is seen as more than a mere provider of resources.
- The members of the local congregation do not regard themselves as autonomous but look for a representative body such as the diocese or district to manage its relations with wider society.
- The district, province or diocese provides a context in which to function. It is not just a business relationship.
- Such a view presupposes a leader ministry provided from a wider context who is willing to accept representative functions.
- A bishop, moderator or chairman is seen as a symbol for the denomination. They are willing to accept good and bad projections. Words to describe them such as Shepherd and Father in God are acceptable.
- The wider community may look to its bishop as a parish looks to its vicar.

An *associational congregation* will display a range of quite different characteristics and have a more detached relationship with its local community and with its denomination (see Figure 2.2).

- It will be less conscious of its local community and vice versa.
- Members may assemble and disperse from a wide area.
- Ministers will make less attempt to visit non-members.
- It assesses the effectiveness of its ministry in the willingness of people to attend more regularly.
- Ministers are a part of the congregation, 'one of them', authority is seen to come from within the group rather than from outside.
- Members expect to support their congregation by sacrificial financial giving.
- Social activities are encouraged within the congregation and discouraged outside.

Congregations with these associational characteristics will also have a different view of their relationship to their wider denomination.

- The diocese or district will be seen as an administrative machine.

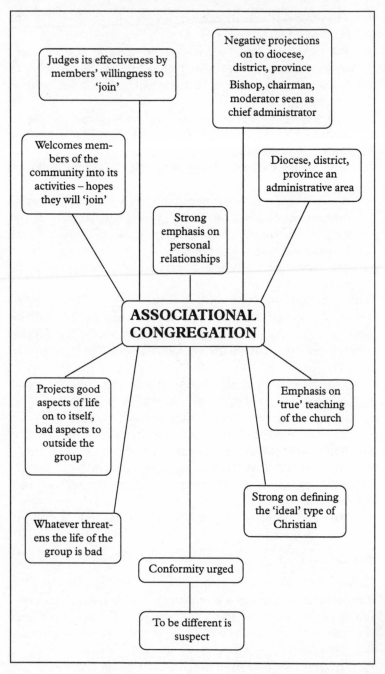

Figure 2.2   Associational congregations

- The value of the wider grouping will be seen in providing support for specialist services, theological training and legal services.
- The congregation, while willing to pay its share, really wants to be left alone to supply its ministry from within.
- The district or diocese is seen as a threat to the congregation's own internal control.
- The bishop or chairman is seen as an administrator and as a symbol of the collective fellowship of a group of independent congregations. Primarily negative projections are given.
- Within the Anglican Communion such congregations feel constrained by the traditions of Anglican practice. They want to be more like Congregational or Roman Catholic congregations but not to accept the disciplines of another denomination.

Those extreme pictures of the different ways in which congregations can behave will seem exaggerated. To some they will be descriptions which bring a wry smile about how other congregations behave. There will be elements of both in many congregations. The most helpful piece of recognition is to understand what is going on in the corporate life of this group of people. Many of the terrific arguments which blow up within local communities and within congregations stem either from a new minister coming who sees things differently, or from a group growing in influence in a congregation who want to move more in one direction and disturb the present balance. Sensitive management is needed to hold together the tension created by pressure from different groups. Vision is required to understand what might be right for this community at this stage of its life.

Size does make a difference

In Alan Ecclestone's world of the church in England of the 1940s and 1950s it was quite normal for one clergyman to look after one or perhaps two parishes. He would know almost everyone in the congregation quite well and they would understand what he was there for. Today, almost everywhere in England, such a picture is impossible to sustain. Urban, inner-city ministry has taken on patterns of its own, rural ministry is frequently about 'sharing' one priest or minister between three, four or five congregations. Suburban ministry is often about managing congregations of 200 people or more without the support available in Victorian or Edwardian times of several curates, a smattering of layworkers and, according to tradition and denomination, a community of religious sisters. There is no one job description or way of seeing a vicar. Nor is there one way of understanding the life and dynamics of a congregation. Size and situation are important. It is right now to look at an influential piece of analysis which has been done by Roy Oswald of the Alban Institute and to add to it and adapt it for situations other than that of the congregations of the United States.[5] It has rung bells wherever I have shared ideas about congregations, from the smallest village church in the Yorkshire Dales to the most able of clergy in Scandinavia.

Family-, pastoral-, programme- and corporate-sized congregations

Basing his analysis on previous work done by Arlin Rothauge, Oswald sets out four basic congregational sizes. Each presents specific sets of behaviour from its members and each requires different methods of working from its ministers. None are absolutely watertight. Some appear to function well even though they are in the wrong category, but life is full of exceptions. I have to add a fifth category to take into account the demands made on clergy with more than one parish and for congregations who share one minister. I also want to say something about the relatively new phenomenon of 'church planting'.

The small or 'family'-sized congregation
The Diocese of Ely in the east of England declared 1994 'The year of the small church'. It was a deliberate attempt to support the small congregation, to affirm the work of the clergy in such places and to celebrate what can be achieved. All too easily small congregations are seen as problems, as ripe for closure or joining with neighbouring parishes, as prey to ideas about teams or groups. Clergy can feel undervalued when offered 'charge' of such small congregations. They can be seen as places for the sick, for pre-retirement placements or to be shared with an appointment to a specialist ministry.

What has hardly ever been attempted is an analysis of the life and needs of clergy and people in the small congregation of 40 people or fewer.

St Ebb's certainly does not exist and these characters are completely unreal; or are they? Eric is the organist, he really only likes hymns and tunes from 'the old book'. He *will* play the new ones, but usually in the style of 'Abide With Me', tune *Eventide*, (10.10.10) slow. After a life in the building trade he distrusts all builders and has no concept at all that architects are useful or that they should be paid a fee. Edna is the person who raises great amounts of money through her jumble sales and the like. She has many helpers but they are 'her friends' and most do not come to church. Newcomers are said to be welcome but often find that they have not been given a place behind a stall or a job to do at the next social event.

Or let us look at St Thomas's, which prides itself on its ritual. It has a tiny congregation of faithful people. Ted is a towering man made even larger in cassock and decorated surplice. If he does not know about it in a service, and agree with it, then either it will not happen or he will cause so much disruption at key moments that whatever is tried is likely to fail. Tessa does the flowers. For some reason she seems to feel she owns every space in church where flowers might go. She protects those spaces, even when empty in Advent or Lent, when there are no flowers at all.

Most of us will recognize some of these behavioural characteristics from congregations we have known. They are, of course, fictitious but my wife and I often remark how there are the same people in our various congregations; they just have different names! Roy Oswald calls this a family-sized church where there are definite and identifiable characteristics.

The family church with patriarchs and matriarchs
This congregation functions like a family and has appropriate parental figures. There characters defend and control the life of the congregation. They feel a responsibility for its survival and need to preserve and keep traditions which generations of previous patriarchs and matriarchs have thought important.

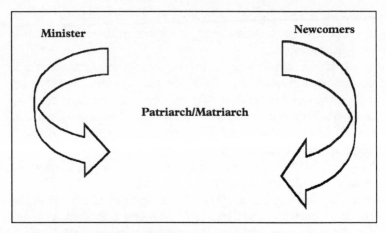

Figure 2.3   A congregation with patriarchs and matriarchs

Defence and survival
Attitudes which are stated as necessary to keep the church open
are the very ones which may be contributing to its downfall. So
much hard work is being put in by so few that it is difficult for
newcomers to get in at all. The key role of the patriarch or matri-
arch is to see that clergy do not take the surviving congregation
off in new directions.

The need for traditional care
These congregations need and expect traditional pastoral care.
The minister has to visit all those in the congregation on a regular basis and be available at all times for crises and demands of
any kind.

Clergy succeed when they consult
Confrontation will lead to disaster. The only way for a minister
to make any progress is to take the needs of the congregation
seriously and to listen to what is being said. However difficult,
befriending the key people is the only way forward.

Clergy are not taken seriously
Deeply-rooted patriarchal and matriarchal congregations survive by not taking their clergy seriously. 'He or she will only be
here for a few years. We can ride their enthusiasms and then go
back to what we know when they move on.'

Clergy do not stay

Small congregations are seen as short-stay first appointments or as a last resting place before retirement. Such placement policies by denominations reinforce what these congregations already know – that they are not being taken seriously. Curates are not trained to handle small congregations. They come from 'successful', often suburban, training parishes. They find it hard to work and to stay with the small congregation because their criteria for what works well lie elsewhere.

The pastoral-sized church

Many people see the congregation with 40 to 130 members as the ideal kind of church. It is the one which is big enough to get things done but small enough for people to know one another by their first names. It is the congregation which will grow most easily by careful attention from the minister who, if they have a mind to, can get around and visit everyone – occasionally! This is the congregation in which training courses can work and where there are just enough people to be able to keep the rotas going. There is enough pledged income to be able to budget and to pay the bills. It is the size looked upon favourably by most denominations as 'successful'. However, all concerned are perplexed that this congregation finds it difficult to grow any larger. The benefits of this size of congregation and the demands made upon all concerned go a long way to explain the dilemma.

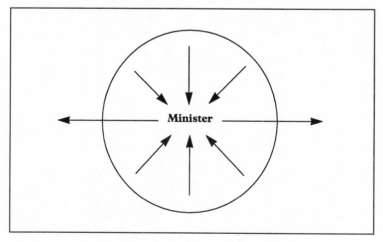

Figure 2.4 The pastoral congregation

The minister relates to everyone

Clergy are usually at the centre of a pastoral church. There are so many parental figures around that they want a central person to be the focus for them.

Personal expectations are high

Everyone has an expectation that they will have some kind of personal relationship with the minister. Visiting is expected. Lay people are encouraged to share in the visiting but the real visit is from the vicar. He or she will be expected to be present at every function, or at least to pay a visit.

Growth depends on the minister's popularity

Within a narrow band, compared with the size of the parish, the congregation will add 20–30 people, or lose them, depending on the popularity of the minister. What happens then is up to the skills and resourcefulness of minister and people.

Oppressive demands are felt

As a congregation grows to 100 the personal demands on the minister become enormous. No one person can cope with the individual expectations of so many people. Delegate or die.

The person at the centre

It is the minister who is the focus of the congregational community. He or she is seen as primarily responsible for recruitment, whether or not this is true. Newcomers can expect to get a personal visit from the minister who is also the principal shepherd of newcomers into the congregation by making invitations and ensuring that they are put on rotas. Present job-holders might move aside if the minister asks.

Hard on the minister's family

The minister's family often say that they feel they are in a sharing agreement with the rest of the congregation. The strains on a marriage are enormous. Great care has to be taken to give time to the family and to get time off together.

Size is a block to growth

The greatest problem in congregations of this size is to be able to overcome their minister-focused orientation. Delegation and genuine shared ministries are a must. Lay teams of visitors are essential. Lay leaders need to be identified and trained. A new relationship has to be negotiated with the minister – preferably before heart attack, breakdown or divorce.

The 'cluster' of congregations

Somewhere between the family and the pastoral congregation levels, each relating to one minister, is another common situation. This is where several parishes and congregations are brought together with one minister. Much more learning needs to be done about these situations, although there have now been some interesting pieces of work done on rural groupings, not least in my own Diocese of Bradford in a series of publications on collaborative ministry called *Varieties of Gifts*.[6] More formally this situation applies to teams and groups, but here more clergy are involved. Several years of work with ministers and people in these clusters has led to the production of this check-list of essentials to be taken into account.

The Church of England report *Faith in the Countryside*, published in 1990, has on almost its last page one of those 'busy' diagrams which anyone who lives and worships in a parish where there is more than one church, a team or a group, will recognize and with which they will have the utmost sympathy!

Some key pointers about how to survive in these situations are necessary. They come from the experience of practitioners and can be described in a diagram like the one in Figure 2.5.

- Always get help with administration. One secretary for all the units can save much frustration. A computer helps enormously with data, lists and in producing the group newsletter.
- Clarify the expectations of the congregations. Do they realize the minister is not theirs exclusively? How much time per week can be given to each congregation? Delegate all local responsibilities. Agree how expenses will be shared.
- Streamline the pattern of meetings. Avoid duplication wherever possible. Encourage gradual co-operation. Establish a regular pattern of services in a month. Services which are at the same time every Sunday help people to get into a routine and to remember when to come.
- Decide on a regular day of the week to visit in each

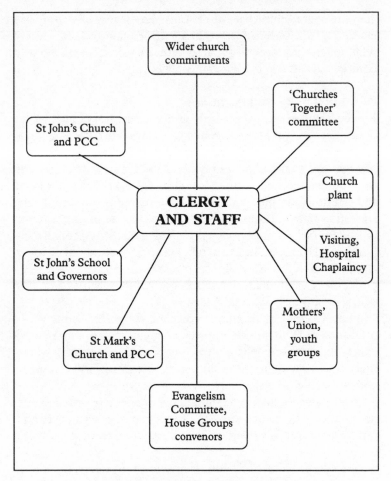

Figure 2.5 The cluster of congregations

community. This also avoids jealousy about where the minister spends time.

• Let everyone know who the local person is for contacts about weddings, baptisms and funeral details.

• Make full use of meeting rooms for local events in each community. Encourage people to travel to support each other's special events.

• Make great use of the fifth Sunday in a month for times of united worship.

• Ensure everyone in each community knows that the vicarage, manse, presbytery is equally theirs. Make it clear how the minister and family want to use it as a public place, if at all.

- It is vital that the minister knows who is related to who in the different communities.
- Get to know the history of co-operation or rivalry between the different communities.
- Understand where the joint meeting places for communities are – schools, Guides and Scouts, Women's Institutes, Rotary, etc. Do not clash or duplicate.

The 'programme' congregation

Much has been written – almost too much – about the ceiling of 150 or so people which many congregations with one minister appear to reach. I think that there is a real, and very understandable, sense in which the human-sized congregation or group of people does not want to grow so large that people do not know each other by their Christian names. In a later section I shall suggest that one of the reasons for the appropriateness of church planting is so that congregations can be kept to this human size.

The so-called 'programme' congregation is one which has managed to break through the numbers ceiling and establish an acceptable new structure. The fundamentally different characteristic of this congregation is that there has been acceptance gained for high quality personal contact with the minister, to be supplemented by other methods of pastoral care. Lay visitors, support and discussion groups and a devolved, lay-led, management structure take the place of the omni-competent minister. A programme congregation will have many of these characteristics:

- Several staff members, ordained and lay.
- A well-developed lay leadership who can work well with the staff team. Concepts of what 'collaborative ministry' is have been explored.
- The principal minister is still central but the role and expectations have been changed. Sometimes a present minister can manage the change as growth takes place. Often illness or strain forces it. A new minister can negotiate and be happier with a different style.
- Good administration takes on a more publicly acknowledged role. The need for systems to assist recruiting,

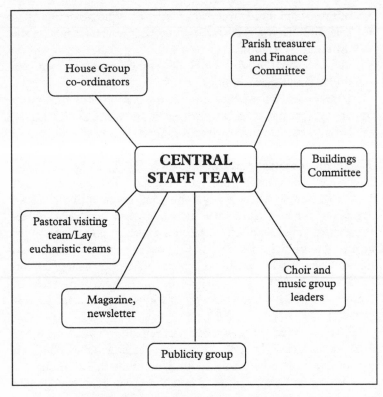

Figure 2.6 The programme congregation

planning, co-ordinating, training, co-ordinating and evalu-
ating become obvious.

• One of the principal roles of the minister is to be the pastor
to the lay leaders and to help groups arrive at a consensus
around a shared vision.

• 'Unless clergy can learn to derive satisfaction from the work
of pastoral administration, they should think twice about
accepting the call to such a parish' (Roy Oswald).

The 'corporate' congregation

Large, famous, eclectic, congregations are corporate churches.
People attend for a whole range of different reasons from those
which attract others to the small, local congregation. Here
preaching and the ecclesiastical tradition are important. Such a
church may function as a symbol of a particular kind of worship
for many others. Congregation members would not expect the

principal minister to visit them. Associate ministers and a staff team will have responsibility for all of the day-to-day running of the church. Lay leaders and salaried professionals will be responsible for specialized areas of work such as music, pastoral counselling and publishing.

The corporate congregation will have many of these features:

- High priority will be placed on the quality of the special kind of worship which is being offered.
- Preaching will be very important. Sermons are likely to be recorded and sold.
- The musical tradition will be of a very high quality.
- The staff team spend significant time on sermons and the preparation of worship.
- The senior minister is a symbol of unity and stability.
- The staff team will be collegial but diverse in skills.
- The leadership team will generate energy and momentum for the congregation.

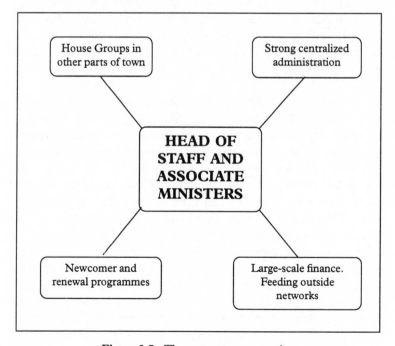

Figure 2.7   The corporate congregation

- A very dispersed congregation will be supported by a sophisticated computerized system and a range of new-member
  and renewal programmes.
- The methods of contacting, and following up, newcomers
  will be very sophisticated.
- This church is a large-scale financial operation which feeds
  and supports a range of associated networks doing similar
  work.

The 'church plant' congregation

One of the most interesting and attractive ideas following the
growth in numerical size of a congregation is that where some of
the members are deliberately shaved off to form a new community. This is called 'church planting' and has spawned a growth
industry of literature all of its own. So many church plants have
taken place now in Britain that wisdom and experience are
emerging. There is no doubt that a great amount of stress also
accompanies this activity!

The classic, and most enduring, church plants are those
where a junior or associate minister moves away from the
larger congregation and inhabits different premises with some
members of the parent congregation. Evidence has shown that
the numbers of those 'lost' to the original congregation are soon
made up with further new members and that resources are bare-
ly depleted, if at all.

Those who move over to the baby church are highly moti-
vated and display many of the characteristics described in my
section on the 'life cycle' of a congregation in its infancy phase
(see page 47). There is a high level of energy, there appear to be
too few people and too few hours in the day to complete all the
perceived tasks, and as a consequence there is a ready and open
welcome for newcomers. Since the minister and some of the
congregation have come from a known congregation there is a
strong sense of support from a group close by. Feelings of isolation and bereavement are at a very low level.

One of the major questions surrounding a church plant is the
choice of a new building. In many urban examples a church in a
neighbouring community which has become very weak is 'taken
over'. Contrary to some expectations, such a move has often
been seen as a welcome innovation and not as an oppressive
monopolizing. Newcomers come with fresh energy and a

renewed vision. They do not always come with the same brand of churchmanship, and respect for the minority has to be a key concern.

Indeed, the establishment of an appropriate level of church order can be a real problem for the 'planted' congregation. Many have come from the more evangelical wing of a denomination and sit lightly to tradition and liturgical order in their own understanding of church. The minister who travels with a group into a plant can be both a liberator and an order-giver in such situations. It is often the second minister in a plant who brings the new order and consolidation. I well remember hearing of the frustration of one bishop going to a confirmation in a church plant in a former warehouse. He said that that he had some difficulty in finding the Holy Table and, once found, had to lay his crozier or shepherd's crook on the floor because no one had thought about where he would place his things on this more formal occasion!

Church plants are with us and they are exciting. In England during the 1990s more churches were opened than were closed and this in itself is a great testimony to the vitality of many congregations. For this study the great lesson learned by having church plants is that they enable a congregational group to retain that relatively personal size where each member can relate to the minister and to one another without feeling lost in the crowd. They are a very real way in which the pastoral-sized church can be retained and duplicated but where exponential growth can be continued. This is the human-sized Christian community which seems to be preferred by many.

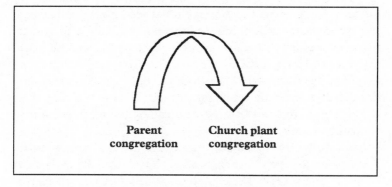

Figure 2.8 The church plant congregation

In the relatively new world of church planting there are many variations on what a church plant will look like and what its origins will be. Martin Robinson and David Spriggs in their training manual *Church Planting* have described ten different types of plant.[7]

1. *The daughter church.* This is the time-honoured way of establishing a new, initially dependent, congregation from an original 'mother' church.
2. *The 'strawberry runner'.* In this situation there is no expectation that a new church will become independent. It will always serve as an adjunct to the principal congregation.
3. *Planting by colonization.* In this situation a number of church members may be sent out to establish a new, small community. They may begin in a house or a community room.
4. *Planting by adoption.* There are occasions where an existing group will invite another congregation to take over its work. The adopted group looks to their chosen mother church to provide vision, direction, leadership and sometimes additional resources of money. Some 'shared building' congregations look like this.
5. *Planting by producing multiple congregations.* In this situation congregations of different kinds use the same building but with no intention of forming one overall congregation with a common identity.
6. *Planting by accident.* Such church plants come about as a result of a split in the congregation. Hopefully, no one plans church planting by schism!
7. *Planting by mission team.* A deliberate and planned effort can create a new congregation where none has existed before. A team from other congregations or from an agency can establish this type of plant, which requires careful planning and long nurture.
8. *Planting by pioneer.* There are talented individuals who are called, almost by temperament, to this work. Often they move on after a plant, or new congregation, is becoming consolidated.
9. *Planting with a founding pastor.* Some clergy are called to encourage new congregations. Other clergy may only support one plant in their lifetime. A new housing estate is a common place for such clerical work to be done.

10. *Planting by crusade or mission.* A high-profile event, with much publicity and planning, can draw local people into the commitment to begin a new congregation in an area of need or where there has been a change of population.

Beware: a family health warning

Many congregational commentators have now come across this family, pastoral, programme, corporate way of describing congregations. Numerous articles and books have been published by authors who think that if they can re-tell the analysis in an anecdotal way then they have revealed a Holy Grail for their readers. Sadly, many of these writers are among the most deceived. They have described symptoms and rehearsed conclusions, but they have not understood the restructuring needed to ensure that lasting change will take place.

One basic assumption needs to be understood. I can illustrate it best by referring to research done by an Alban Institute writer. This comes from a stimulating article on congregational revitalization by Gill Rendle. It is that 'if congregations want growth or revitalization, they will have to change their systems – their structures, the way they "get on" with one another – if they are going to grow and develop in ways which are right for them'.[8]

There is a level of discovery about congregational revitalization which says that we have to discover our congregations as systems and manage them as such. The alternative is to dilute or overburden ourselves in trying to address the multiple needs of an increasingly diverse group of people who surround the minister and the pastoral team. To continue in this way is still to be looking for the solution at the wrong end of the problem.

To ask questions about *who we are* is much more difficult than to look at *what we should do next*. In fact, congregations often fall into the trap of 'doing something' as a way of avoiding the more difficult question of understanding themselves and their particular call to ministry. For a congregation to be able to move from any one of our categories to another requires an understanding of what kind of a community they are now. Often when I was asked to work with congregations in London I would begin with the question 'Do you really understand what it will be like if the change you say you want really comes about?' They know they want to grow a little in numbers, but they actually want a few more people to join who will be 'just like them'. Unfortunately (or fortunately?) few such people exist. If congregations grow, and continue to grow, structural, organizational changes have to take place. Without this understanding, anguish and strife arise. The programme for growth in our church is pronounced a failure. Either the consultants are blamed or the local community for being unresponsive, when in fact the present not-understood system was so powerful that it could resist all unthinking attempts to modify it. When systems are understood and structures changed with an intelligent understanding of the consequences, then there is no going back.

More than survival means the exciting opportunity to look at why your congregation is as it is. With the idealism of an Ecclestone, the question 'What might it be like?' can be asked. With the analysis of interested people and of organizations like the Grubb and Alban Institutes it is possible to describe where your church is in relation to its local community, and perhaps to God.

There is always a 'beyond survival'. It might mean the dispersal of a community or the amalgamation of congregations after a building has closed. It might mean a new life discovered when the theology, assumptions and systems which hold a congregation are brought into the revealing light of day. A door will have been opened which will allow a congregation, and its members at their own pace, to make tentative new steps towards horizons still shrouded in the mist of God's glory. A congregation will be able to understand itself a little better and begin to be able to move on from what it is, towards its dreams of what it might become.

Notes

1   For an extended study on this theme see Christopher P. Burkett, 'A leadership that deals with meanings: appreciating the power of organizational culture in congregations' in John Nelson (ed.), *Managing and Leading* (Canterbury Press, 1998).

2   Alan Ecclestone, *Staircase for Silence* (Darton, Longman and Todd, 1997), p. 77.

3   Charles E. Smith, 'Leadership and strategic intent: the Merlin factor', *Harvard Business Review* (1991); reproduced with permission.

4   Giles Ecclestone (ed.), *The Parish Church* (Mowbrays, 1988).

5   Roy M. Oswald, 'How to minister effectively in family, pastoral,

program and corporate sized churches', *Action Information* (Alban Institute, March/April 1991).

6   *Varieties of Gifts Towards a Viable and Effective Ministry for the 21st Century*, Diocese of Bradford, Cathedral Hall, Stott Hill, Bradford BD1 4ET.

7   Martin Robinson and David Spriggs, *Church Planting: The Training Manual* (Lynx Communications, 1995).

8   Gill Rendle, 'Congregational revitalization: there's nothing more practical than theory', *Inside Information* (Alban Institute, Spring 1995).

3

Understanding
Growth and Decline

Change does not take place just because an interesting piece of analysis or clever interpretation of a congregation has been completed. Before a congregation will change its nature, careful pastoral care and some first steps to give new experiences is needed. I always enjoy carrying out a light-hearted but serious 'health check' when beginning new work with members of a congregation. What is used is an adaptation of a grid which I first came across in *The Parish as a Learning Community* by Thomas Downs.[1] I ask members of the group to award their congregation points on two scales. One is for how friendly or caring their congregation is. The other is for how good they are at getting work done in their congregation. A score of 1–9 is used. The grid is reproduced below.

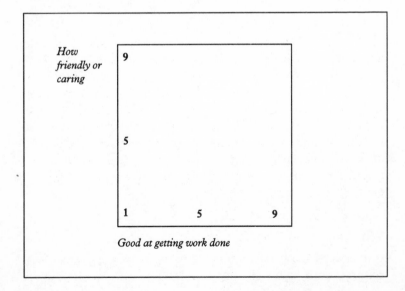

Good at getting work done

Each member is asked to work individually. When everyone is finished I ask members to call out their 'scores'. Each individual's response is given a mark on the grid which I have drawn out on a large sheet of paper. This causes great hilarity but many serious things are said in the reporting back.

I then flip the paper over and show Downs' analysis of such scores. This is the next diagram.

Congregational life

Bowls Club congregation (1–9)	Collaborative congregation (9–9)
Weak congregation (1–1)	Hyperactive congregation (9–1)

Congregational mission

I then add my own analysis that unless a parish has most of its 'scores' in the area of the grid 4–4 and above, then that congregation is not ready for real change. Delicate and early measures have to be used in the congregation which is either too nice and too caring to get anything done or too insensitive in its programmes that whatever is decided is done irrespective of the feelings of the victims! When a congregation's activities and its life are thought to have 4–4 and above characteristics then a sufficient degree of sharing in ministry exists for there to be real dialogue about any possible changes.

What is it that prevents growth?

If such participative methods of working are readily available to congregations, and if the baptismal calling is becoming central to each of us, why is it that open congregations are not the most common feature of our churches? If all the members of a congregation could be of a similar mind and at a similar stage in their growth, then such a dream might become a possibility. The truth is that, even within one congregation, various members and groups are at different stages in their life. Some are vibrant and new, full of enthusiasm. Others are on a plateau but are very comfortable with their situation. They may not know that they are at the peak of their activity. Many would feel, to us clergy at least, to be in a terminal state of decline, well past any hope of visible baptismal regeneration.

The independent Swedish Christian adult education agency Svenska Kirkya Studiesbund produced a most engaging cover to its publications catalogue a few years ago. This showed a man climbing the staircase of life. He began on the early steps as a child, a young man and as an adult. At the top of the stairs he was a fully-grown man, and as he descended steps on the other side he became older. The point of the lovely drawing was not the fatalism of 'We are born, we suffer and we die' but to emphasize that all the stages of life are times when we can learn and grow and where real change is possible.

The life and death of congregations

At something of the same time that I saw this drawing my interest grew in an article which crossed the Atlantic in the Alban Institute journal. It described just this situation: that in any organization, the various groups and members of it are each at different stages in their 'life cycle'. If an enthused group can have sufficient influence, then renewal can take place. Other groups at different stages in their lives can have other influences. This is a good opportunity to set out the 'Life Cycle of a Congregation' as described by Martin F. Saarinen – adapted, of course, for use also in non-American countries.[2]

The 'gene structure' of a congregation

In a quite fascinating way Saarinen describes how his own thinking came together through reading a series of articles about how some congregations grow and how others appear to decline. In describing his own idea of a congregation's 'life cycle', he says that this cycle has little to do with chronological time. It is to do with what he calls the balance of 'gene structures' common to congregational life.

There are four energizing factors.

The E-factor is concerned with energizing a congregation or group. It is strong in the early stages of the life of a new congregation or project. It is the glint in the eye of its originators.

The P-factor is for programmes and schemes. A congregation which is going to become stabilized and grow will need to be organized. There have to be groups to oversee the giving, the choir, adult, youth and children's work, the building, visiting and much more.

The A-factor is concerned with intentionality. This is the way in which a congregation expresses its identity in the form of mission statements, goals, objectives or budgets. This thinking will determine how the human resources of a congregation can be used most efficiently and effectively.

The I-factor is for inclusion. It relates to how individuals and groups are drawn into a congregation and assimilated by it into membership. Do the aims of the existing congregation match the needs of those new members who want to come and join? How is power distributed? How is conflict handled? A congregation with a high I-factor is one which is characterized by warmth and friendliness. Theirs is an intimate God whose presence is immanent in the relationships and patterns which open and close doors to those coming into the congregation.

The ascent scale of a life cycle

Birth

The major characteristic of a young congregation or group is that it has high levels of energy and enthusiasm and that it is integrated around an idea or the vision and charisma of a founder. People are so enthusiastic that there are not sufficient members to support all the ideas which bubble up. They cannot understand why others do not wish to rush and join them. There is a prime need to broaden the membership.

Infancy

The high quality of personal relationships matches the levels of enthusiasm which everyone has. People enjoy working together for a common aim. There is an open and unrestricted inclusiveness for all who want to come and join. Programmes are undeveloped and not thought through but no one really minds. There is some initial frustration as a few people drift away when they decide this kind of 'fellowship' is not for them. Time has to be given to continue to develop a high sense of community and mission. Specific ministries begin to develop.

Adolescence

This congregation has a 'busy bee' culture. Levels of energy are high but are focused on the systematic development of the organization. Everyone is very busy doing something. Unrealistic idealism which characterized earlier stages tends to be dismissed. There is early conflict over purposes and mission. The founder finds a dilemma. Often the early leaders decide to leave or take a back seat. The founder minister begins to suffer from stress or 'burn-out' and may decide this is the time to hand over to someone with different skills. Membership needs to be broadened and space found within activities for people with a range of interests and understandings of faith.

Prime

Here is the large congregation which begins to know that it is 'successful'. There is a strong interaction between the inner and outer life of the members. Intentionality and inclusion correspond. Programmes and vision are attractive. The responsibilities of the minister and congregation members complement each other. There is high pastoral and corporate responsibility. The dangers of the dominance of one group begin to emerge. Skills have to be developed to try to resolve conflicts. Overall this church still knows where it is going. New members are allowed in. Visitors come from other congregations to see how it is done. Features appear in church newspapers. Commitment and levels of financial giving are high.

The descent scale

Maturity

It is hard to distinguish between prime and maturity. I use the example of people saying 'What did we do last time?' to distinguish the difference. As soon as good times are wanted to be kept

Maturity
Status quo culture. Well-established structures, good administration and staffing, office, administrator. Energetic but unenthusiastic – 'What did we do last time?' Problem of lack of response to new ideas and opportunities. People can join if they want to be like us. Can the mission be rediscovered?

Aristocracy
'Bowls Club' culture. Busy but unenergetic. Efficient and strong fellowship among insiders, exclusiveness, dwindling base of support. Over-extended structures, loss of mission. Can the sense of God's living presence be regenerated?

Bureaucracy
Disillusioned with the rest of the church culture. Golden age a thing of the past. Strong sense of boundaries and own territory. Rigidity, muteness, defensiveness, hostility, suspicion. Personalizing of systemic problems. Can a new identity be discovered with the present people; can newcomers be allowed in?

Death
Artefact culture. Disintegration, despair, loss of memory, identity, hope. Absorption into another ecclesiastical world which no one else can enter. No new life beyond, ultimate power given to closure and death. Start all over again with rebirth and newly energized people.

Prime
Wisdom culture. High interaction between congregation and community. Established programmes but still growing. Conflict is creative, corporate responsibility. Problems of lack of solutions, dominance of one group, polarity of opinions. Develop channels of communication – keep them talking to one another!

Adolescence
Busy-bee culture, high energy level focused on development of activities. High commitment and giving. Family feelings of inclusiveness. Problems of leader burn-out or group disintegration. Conflict over purpose and mission. Solved by broadening concepts, leadership and willingness to include others.

Infancy
High commitment and quality of relationships. Open and unrestricted inclusiveness, contagious enthusiasm. Problems of undeveloped programmes, conditional inclusiveness. Disillusionment, some members leave.

Birth
Integrated around the vision and leadership of a founder or renewed group. High levels of enthusiasm. Not enough people to do all the things needed. Worries: not everyone shares the vision, unresponsiveness. Try to broaden support.

Figure 3.1 The life cycle of a congregation (Martin F. Saarinen, Alban Institute. Adapted by Malcolm Grundy)

and changes greeted with caution, then the downward path has begun. There are still well-established membership systems and a good welcome but it is just a little hard to get in if you are different. The same busyness is there, but without the enthusiasm. 'We do this because we always do it.' The high support levels give stability and a high sense of self-worth to members. New opportunities and changed conditions are greeted with caution. The corporate vision needs to be re-stated.

Aristocracy

The difference between a church and a club is hard to define in these congregations. People are still busy but unenergetic. They come to meet their friends and have a good time. People are defensive of their territory and jobs. Status and exclusiveness may be factors. There is a dwindling base of support: new, young members do not join. There is a loss of any sense of mission. There is a need to restore God's sense of purpose through the history of the congregation and a need to generate anew a congregation's awareness of its sense of vocation.

Bureaucracy

People are disillusioned. The golden age of the life of the congregation is no longer sought. People are defensive of their jobs and territory. There is a strong sense of boundaries and a 'muteness' about discussions for change. Hostility and suspicion are rife, and factions vie with each other over issues which are difficult to define – or remember. The structures cannot possibly be changed. Hope exists if the silent or the powerless can be allowed a voice. It is possible to establish a new sense of identity if existing dominant members can see that age and time will prevent them continuing.

Death

Here an 'artifact' culture predominates. Life is about protecting the stones, or the windows, or the statues or the organ. There is despair about the future for the congregation. Alternative uses are considered for the building. Schemes for the absorption of the congregation with another are a possibility and become inevitable. There is no power to give new life. Actions reflect a death wish. Only the establishment of a completely new congregation in the shell of the old will give any future.

Not a life but a process

Fascinating as this study is, it rarely describes what is happening to a congregation through the whole of its life. What is going on within the life of this group of people helps to explain why churches with people attending them survive so well, much better than any comparable voluntary organization. A close look at the stage of life different groups are at in a congregation will help the minister and the church council to make realistic decisions about some groups, and to plan for the future.

If a minister is no more than average in capabilities and if the surrounding population is receptive to Christianity, people will continue to attend. One of the most salutary things about a look at statistics of membership of a congregation is the small variation in membership numbers between what are regarded as good times and those which are bad. A pastoral-sized congregation may only vary between 50 and 120 people in an overall population, probably of thousands. Where the population is in hundreds, especially in rural areas, average attendance is usually much higher, but when things go wrong the changes in attendance are much more marked. What a non-churchgoing people who are not sure if they are Christians or not want, is a sympathetic religious institution which will comfort and care for them at times of crisis and transition. Managing the interaction between the committed and the attached non-attenders is what the dynamic of religion is all about.

Churches survive through the centuries because this function is desperately needed in any society and because the local church has learned how to interpret and express community feeling. Christians believe that through the life, death and resurrection of Jesus they have a way of mediating the experiences of life in a way which speaks to those who are searching. The liturgies and rituals of this church, developed through the centuries, can speak with a richness and resonance available nowhere else. D. H. Lawrence in *The Rainbow* called the church's year with its calendar and rituals 'The epic of the saga of mankind'. He had touched on something very real and had understood the connection which a national and a local church could make with a people.

If this is in any way an accurate supposition about the place of religion in society, then churches and congregations which manage to connect with any people's expression of their need will continue. Life cycles will always be there and need to be understood. Churches die and congregations come to an end for other reasons. There is both a stubbornness and an unwillingness to accept how and why congregations die.

Four reasons why congregations die

1. They are in the wrong place

Quite simply, demographic movements can kill off a congregation. With the fluidity of population movements in post-industrial communities, housing estates can be razed and populations moved as planners and developers move in. Many inner-city and city centre churches have suffered for no other reason than that nobody lives around there any more.

There are two significant variations on this theme. One is that developed by Professor Robin Gill in a number of his books but worked out with comprehensive research in *The Myth of the Empty Church*.[3] It is that populations were at their maximum or declining before large new churches were built. In a series of studies in the north east of England he has shown that some ambitious church buildings were never able to attract the congregations for which they were designed. There were simply not enough potential churchgoers around. The consequence of this was that some churches were never more than half-full. Realistically, they actually looked, and felt, half-empty. Such situations were demoralizing from the outset. Newcomers felt that they were part of a losing show and went away. Congregations found themselves saddled with enormous debts and were handicapped from useful work and evangelistic activity by the obligation to raise funds for themselves. Some congregations are always asking for money.

The other variation contradicts the demographic argument. It is that congregations will travel for the kind of worship they want. Increasingly the concept of the local congregation made up of local people is hard to sustain. The motor car, fast roads and wide ranges of liturgy and church style have made an already mobile population take its mobility into its religious consciousness. To take only one example from my own work area. Bolton Abbey is a ruined Benedictine priory. Twenty years ago the church was given a roof and worship was re-established. The village has a population of 577, the church has a membership roll of 307. The fast A59 road runs through this attractive area of Wharfedale linking main centres of population. Many of the 300 or so worshippers each Sunday drive up to thirty miles for traditional worship, fully choral and very well done, from the 1662 Book of Common Prayer. They do this because what they want is not available locally. In doing so they have created, and sustain through very generous giving, a local centre to provide the kind of worshipping life they need.

2. Dependency is hard to overcome

One of the hardest things to understand about congregations is the relationship which the people have with their minister and the relationship of the congregation to its denomination. This whole area has been explored in considerable depth by Bruce Reed in *The Dynamics of Religion*.[4] Deep levels of unconscious behaviour are at play here. When things go wrong and expectations cannot be fulfilled then bitterness and recrimination result. Denominations too can be both patronizing and controlling. When such a relationship becomes oppressive a congregation finds it hard to survive. It appears to derive no vitality from its own life and cannot renew itself. Some congregations are subsidized by their denominations for a wide range of reasons, but the ultimate result is the demise of a congregation, albeit delayed for a few years.

Some ministers thrive on dependency. They are probably unaware of this because they may have flourishing churches. The telling time comes when they depart or retire. The congregation proves to be founded on the needs of one person and has not been encouraged to develop a life of its own. Try as they might, the next minister cannot establish themselves or prise people away from the memory of their previous minister.

As Bruce Reed states, dependency understood and worked with is a fundamental part of a person's religious needs. They oscillate between states of dependence and independence. The mistake the unwitting or egocentric minister makes is to confuse the dependency on God with a displaced dependency on themselves.

3. Authority is hard to own for ourselves

Recent years have seen denominations unable to cope with their internal divisions. Most recently this has been the situation for the Church of England over the decision to ordain women. In the Roman Catholic Church differences are stretched to the limit over teaching in some of the Encyclicals and over the question of celibacy. What is happening there has been a feature of churches and congregations through the centuries. Usually over questions of doctrine and principle, congregations have seceded from the parent church. When only one congregation goes, or a group of individuals, then the breakaway lasts only for the lifetime of those who go. Where a more sizable group break away, then continuing churches survive. Some of these appear to have teaching which is somewhat in a time-warp.

In our own time it is the question of authority which causes so much resentment. Congregations need a parent body. Bishops and chairmen or moderators can function as a focus for unity and as a place where projections and anger can go. Authority today too often appears to be caught up with the defence of a position which time and events have overtaken. This was more possible in days when communication was slow; but in today's fast-moving world, churches have to think and pronounce with speed and knowledge if they are to have any credibility.

Authority is also called into question when the teachings of a church are not kept by a sizeable number of its members. Such disowning attacks the integrity of any denomination. When the only real authority a church has is of a moral nature, it has to rely on its members to live according to its teachings. Part of the reason for the decline of the position of Christianity in our developed countries is that its teachings appear no longer to carry weight even among adherents. A 'lay reformation' has taken place which many clericalized professionals are unwilling to acknowledge.

4. Interdependence is hard to accept

Parochialism is more often than not regarded as a dirty word. It has all the connotations of congregations not wanting to accept that they are part of a greater whole. The unfortunate 'Abdication revealer', Bishop Blunt of Bradford, in one of his most profound charges told his clergy that a diocese was necessary if for no other reason than to prevent congregations lapsing into parochialism!

Congregations eventually go into a decline if they determinedly cut themselves off from any wider fellowship, or from the pastoral support of their denomination. In these days when differences of church order are even more marked and when congregations pay so much for the maintenance of their own ministry, there is an even greater pull towards wanting to be in complete self-control.

There is a growing body of evidence from experiments in 'clustering' that congregations can gain considerable strength by pooling resources. More effective training courses can be organized, better speakers can be enticed – and worship can be much more inspiring when more than a handful of people are trying to sing in a building designed for a crowd. Such collaboration differs from ideas about teams and groups. It is willing, it is voluntary, it is local and it takes no one's independence away. Where such a willingness to work together does not exist already, over-stretched people with limited time available cannot provide all the support and maintainance which a local community and its building may well need.

Dying with honour

As a significant, if somewhat ironic, ending to this section I was delighted to read Gill Rendle's comments on systems and the declining congregation. When a congregation determines to end its life this need not necessarily be a sign of failure. In fact, I am aware of a number of religious orders who have determined on just this path.

Perhaps it is even more critical for churches that have experienced a long, slow period of decline to understand themselves as systems. Like so many churches that have maintained traditional practices, they may actually be designed to decline in a time that has changed so many of our lifestyle behaviours and assumptions. Rather than blame and point fingers, it would be healthier to acknowledge that they are successful in what they are designed to do, i.e, to get older and smaller.[5]

Notes

1   Thomas Downs, *The Parish as a Learning Community* (Paulist Press, 1979), pp. 41, 42.
2   Martin F. Saarinen, 'The life cycle of a congregation', *Action Information* (Alban Institute, May/June 1986).

3   Robin Gill, *The Myth of the Empty Church* (SPCK, 1993).
4   Bruce Reed, *The Dynamics of Religion* (Darton, Longman and Todd, 1978).
5   Gill Rendle, 'Congregational revitalisation', *Inside Information* (Alban Institute, Spring 1995), p. 4.

4

Understanding Collaborative Ministry

Collaborative ministry is certainly central to the thinking of all those who want to see a revitalization of congregational life. Three pieces of writing have emerged from the English churches in recent times and invite critical consideration. The first of these gives as a basis for collaboration an Anglican way of doing things. A Roman Catholic publication comes new to a collaborative way of working and makes it refreshingly attractive. A third attempts to tell us what collaborative ministry is and largely misses the target. They are illustrative pointers to what collaborative ministry might mean. We all learn in part through getting things right and in part though our mistakes.

While not addressing this question directly, the first piece of writing, the Church of England 'Turnbull Report' about the reform of structures, *Working as One Body*[1] devotes its early chapters to an extended description of the essential 'Anglican' nature of this church. They say that in its essence it is based on a series of collaborative partnerships, a formal one with the State, partnerships with voluntary agencies in this country, partnerships with other denominations, partnerships with voluntary missionary agencies and on the partnership of the Anglican Communion.

The authors claim that the Church of England is able to move easily within these partnership relations because of its essentially collaborative nature. They say that it is a church in which authority is dispersed and as such has always been used to living with the tension of difference. It is a church which has always been influenced, and changed, by talented individuals and the pressure of interest groups. While having Episcopacy as one of its core structures it has developed a way of governing the church by a managed interaction of its different parts – episcopal, synodical and legal.

Episcope (literally 'oversight') involves preserving a synoptic vision of the whole, together with responsibilities for ensuring the co-ordination of each aspect of the mission of the Church . . . To be the people of God means to live in a certain quality of personal, face-to-face relationships, embodying God's reconciliation of all things in Christ, living in the light of God's justice, forgiveness and new life.

A Roman Catholic view

Working at almost the same time, the Roman Catholic Bishops' Conference of England and Wales received and published a report on collaborative ministry called *The Sign We Give*.[2] They have been trying to wrestle with relatively new concepts of a clergy and laity deliberately working together in diocesan and congregational life. Coming from a more overtly hierarchical background, this is a publication inspired by a freshness of approach.

It begins with a reflection on Vatican II where the foundation of collaborative ministry was laid when emphasis was given to the place of lay people in the life of the church. While agreeing that collaborative ministry is hard to define, they begin with the concept of communion:

the ability to co-ordinate all the gifts and charisms of the community, to discern them and put them to good use for the upbuilding of the Church in constant union with the Bishops . . . Collaborative ministry is not only the focus for growth or renewal in the Church today. Rather, it is one way of expressing how the Church renews itself.

The report concedes that some parishes have learned their lessons by going directly for a collaborative approach, while others have begun by working with particular community groups or by listening to those with special concerns such as that of women in the church. In all this there is an important overlap between priestly formation, in-service training, and the movement from an authoritative to a collaborative model of working.

In the section 'Collaborative Ministry: Experience and Theology' there are some helpful attempts at the necessary ingredients for a definition:

- Collaborative ministry is a way of relating and working together which expresses the communion which the church is given and to which it is called.
- Collaborative ministry brings together into partnership people who, through baptism and confirmation, as well as ordination and marriage, have different vocations, gifts and offices within the church.
- Involvement in collaborative ministry demands conscious commitment to certain values and convictions.
- Collaborative ministry begins from a fundamental desire to work together because we are called by the Lord to be a company of disciples, not isolated individuals.
- Collaborative ministry is committed to mission. It is not simply concerned with the internal life of the church. Rather it shows to the world the possibility of transformation, of community and of unity within diversity.

There is then developed a theology of collaborative ministry through the concepts of service based on baptism and confirmation to which all are called – and which is reflected in worship and in action. 'Those who do participate actively begin to discover this theology by doing so. For many others, it continues to remain a closed book.' There is an instructive two-way dialogue which is always taking place between church and world.

The question of authority is faced in two ways: that of the authority of all the baptized, and the authority of orders or office within the church. As collaborative ministry gets into the bloodstream of a congregation there will emerge new images of leadership. The authors were attracted to the idea of leader as 'moderator of the aspirations, plans and priorities of a community, always holding the common good before them'. The primary task of the priest is to enable communion to grow rather than 'to run the parish'. There are important concepts here for all denominations. The 'nots' of collaborative ministry are also outlined:

- Not strong lay involvement but little collaboration.
- Not just lay people having parts in the liturgy.
- Not changed structures without consultation in decision-making.

Spread throughout the rest of the report are pointers to the essentials of good practice:

- Collaborative ministry does not happen just because people work together or co-operate in some way. It is a gradual and mutual evolution of new patterns.
- Collaborative ministry is built upon good personal relationships.
- Collaborative teams, where personal relationships are important, highlight the importance of emotional maturity.
- Collaborative parishes and teams generally place a high priority on developing a shared vision, often expressed in a mission statement, or in regularly reviewed aims and objectives.
- The courage to face and work through conflict, negotiating until a compromise is found, and even seeking help in order to resolve it, are not weaknesses but signs of maturity and commitment.
- The desire for shared decision-making is the natural outcome of working collaboratively.
- Some decisions, especially those that set policy or touch on matters of critical importance to the community, can be shared widely and arrived at by consensus.
- Fear among priests and lay people that collaborative ministry will leave them little to do is a major barrier.
- Lack of continuity in ministerial appointments can frustrate collaborative ministry.
- Those working in collaborative teams have to recognize personal and professional boundaries and reconcile these with differing individual situations.
- It is increasingly recognized that men and women characteristically have different ways of communicating and can easily misunderstand each other's needs and intentions.
- Teams need to work very hard at how they communicate, and enable different members to take responsibility for what they think and feel.

A time for sharing?

In something of a contrast to the above, a report from the Church of England Board of Mission also tackled collaborative ministry in *A Time for Sharing: Collaborative Ministry in Mission*.[3] Here, a series of authors give their own essays on what they think collaborative ministry is. One problem is that their method of working does not model a collaborative, or even a co-operative style.

The Introduction makes both a good and a bad start. The good is that as well as baptism being underlined as a basis for all Christian ministry, there is also a working definition:

> But we would like to return to its roots in the Latin, *collaborare* [mis-spelt in their text], meaning 'to work together' and further to extend the concept of collaborative ministry to include not only 'doing' together, but also 'being together', such that collaboration implies a true partnership and sharing in a common task.

The bad start is that the difference between co-operation and collaboration is never fully explored, with the consequence that subsequent authors get very confused about what exactly it is they are commending.

In the section giving a brief theological basis, the contributor touches on God as Trinity, the church as the Body of Christ and the world as the sphere of God's activity. We are given a paragraph on the 'Ordained Ministry as a "Support for all Ministry"'. The basic theological underpinning for collaborative ministry needs to be given here and without it the rest does not seem to cohere. Words like 'support' and 'help' do not go well with concepts of enabling people to escape from dependency. A case needs to be made out even for this model of pastoral, clerical ministry.

We are then told that it is hard to bring collaborative ministry into practice in time of crisis – wait until conditions are not too pressing!

Another contributor has practised community development concepts from his time in South Africa and while he was an Agricultural Chaplain. He writes sensitively, pointing us towards John Taylor's writings in *The Go-between God*. In wonderful contrast to what has gone before we are told that 'To work collaboratively is of the essence of mission. Indeed, those periods in the Church's history when there have been clear movements of growth and outreach, have nearly always been marked by collaborative styles of witness and ministry.' There is a characteristically good chapter by Bishop Tom Butler telling us how we have got to be where we are and why we need collaborative structures in our churches and collaborative methods from our clergy, but he has worked in East Africa and been involved with the Church Urban Fund for many years.

A Time for Sharing begins to get it seriously wrong with the next contribution. On one page 'will need' and 'will be' and other 'will' phrases are used at least six times. I am worried that by the method of writing as well as by what is implied, the sign given is that collaborative ministry is about 'telling' and not about collaborating. It goes on to say: 'Delegation is a crucial part of this style.' Is it really? There is a misunderstanding about 'working together' and about 'being together' which is serious in its implications.

A later contributor also says that collaborative ministry is the same as working together. I do not think so. They describe the 'ship', top-down, system of command and suggests that this is a good basis for collaborative ministry, ending with the remarkable quote: 'The fact that leadership is focused on one person has ensured people know what the team's task is and has enabled them to achieve it. They act as what someone described as "agents of coherence". That seems a good definition.' Perhaps it is for one way of working together, but it is not a definition of collaborative ministry – even as described by other authors in the booklet.

There are then descriptions of local examples of collaborative ministry. With the exception of the story about the work of a group of religious sisters, the examples are, when analysed, much more examples of co-operation. Such co-operation is a very necessary first step, but without reflection on the activity and, as *The Sign We Give* says, 'a conscious commitment to certain values and convictions' it is a way of working which soon gets forgotten in the heat of the day and when pressure comes to a group or organization.

One pearl eventually rolls out of this irritating oyster. As a postscript, Marion Mort gives a meditation on the Rublev Ikon, used as the illustration on the front cover of the booklet. She writes in a sensitive theological way:

> If we attempt to visualize Trinity, we may well imagine a stained glass representation of a cloud-surrounded Father God above an impossibly hovering dove above a crucifix held rigidly vertical in a narrow lancet. The Rublev Icon, however, dissolves this hierarchical structure and presents us with an image of unity, harmony and courtesy, in which no one is dominant.
>
> . . . The persons of the Trinity never act at variance with one another. They work together for the Good. There is no struggle for precedence. It is impossible to withdraw or abstract one member from the Trinity whose Unity is definitive . . . The image of the Rublev Ikon offers us the courteous inclination and attention of the three figures to one another. This is a company that listens as well as speaks, that shares silence as well as conversation, that reflects together on the action that has been taken and that will be taken together.

It is vital for our churches and congregations that this debate about collaborative ministry has been rekindled. It is essential if the churches are to work alongside others in creative partnerships. Congregations which grow are those which have mutual respect and collaboration at the core of their beliefs. Community projects work if they have these concepts as their essence. My surprise is that with the experience which many of us have shared in recent years it is still possible to get basic understandings so wrong. Collaborative ministry is about listening and not telling, it is about partnership and changed authority relationships. It requires a continual process to learning and re-evaluation. It can even change the churches.

Surviving shared ministry

Some of the most over-used words of today are about 'shared ministry'. I have seen them so abused that clergy, especially those who have worked in particularly hierarchical denominations, go completely overboard and abdicate all responsibility and all leadership. One Roman Catholic congregation described it to me as

'Over to you, I am off to the golf course'. I have seen others abuse shared ministry to become just another way of jobs being shared out but with the minister retaining control. Really well-thought-out and applied shared ministry is very like the concept in community development of non-directive leadership. Here a person, working with others, deliberately creates structures where decisions can be made corporately, where responsibility is shared and where people are allowed to grow at their own pace. They can take on responsibilities and leadership when they have tested themselves out and are ready for it.[4] Very similar concepts can be used in church life. It is my firmly-held conviction that no real and lasting growth can take place within a congregation unless these ideas about working non-directively and about what shared leadership is really like are understood and practised. These working methods have firm biblical foundations, not least in the ways that Jesus worked with those who came to him.

Collaborative ministry and congregational development

What is required in our exploration of the relationship between church growth and 'shared ministry' is an understanding of the nature of church life as it is reflected in a changing relationship between minister and people. I want to do this by looking at a series of ways in which ministers can choose to work with their people. These ideas were first developed by my colleague at Avec, Revd Dr Henry Grant SJ. He began this thinking with Base Communities in Paraguay and developed it with a number of pieces of parish work in Britain and Ireland.

It has always been something of a sobering thought to me to have to be reminded that the word 'hierarchy' has its origins in ecclesiastical life. There is something strangely paradoxical that the church of the New Testament and the first centuries, which was so concerned to listen to people and to consult about growth and development, should have turned into such a centralized organization within a few hundred years. It is equally sobering to examine denominations which are in the family of 'Reformed' churches and see how many of them have gradually moved from a situation of freedom and participation to one of central control. Is there something of the fallenness of human nature about all this? Many have seen the need to preserve teaching and tradition by imposing a series of centralized controls.

Can hierarchies be liberating? I believe that they can if they deliberately set out to work in particular ways. I am certain that organizations of a hierarchical nature can be changed by groups within them deliberately choosing to work collaboratively. I want to test out these ideas in a description of particular types of congregation where there has been a policy decision to work participatively. For these descriptions I am relying primarily on the work done by Dr Henry Grant and our work together between 1992 and 1994.

The minister-dominated congregation (Figure 4.1)

A hierarchically structured congregation looks the same in any denomination. The minister does almost everything themselves. That is why they are ministers, it is why they studied and were ordained. The minister 'ministers to' the people. The people want to be ministered to. They are a type of 'clients' to the minister. The attitude of letting themselves be served predominates.

The minister tries to satisfy everyone's wishes. This preoccupation with wanting to please everyone causes many sleepless nights. Each group in the congregation makes its own demands – the minister should visit all the families, should take communion to the sick and should spend time with each old person. The minister has to offer interesting trips for young people, try to reconcile fighting married couples, prepare interesting services, edit the parish newsletter, raise money to repair the church, for the central funds and to give away. And if the minister dies of a heart attack or leaves, it is hoped that the next person will do all that and even more!

The compliant congregation with some participation (Figure 4.2)

Here is the beginning of shared ministry. People begin to share in the work of carrying out the many tasks which need to be done in a parish. There are lively debates in the church council. People are encouraged to form groups to organize tasks, and house groups take place around specific themes. The servers' group meets without the minister, as do the choir and mothers' group. The Adult Catechumenate welcomes newcomers.

Figure 4.1   The minister-dominated congregation

Shared ministry is beginning and the congregation is developing more responsibility for its own life. But where is the minister? Has the role ever been discussed? Is this some new conversion? Have they been away on a course? Unless the change of role for the minister is understood they can appear to be absent from the changes, marginalized, the cause of a vacuum in a key place.

Figure 4.2 The compliant congregation with some participation

A congregation which begins to think (Figure 4.3)

Gradually in the discussion groups, the confirmation preparation, and informally at the social gatherings, congregation
members begin to ask one another what is going on. They begin
to enjoy their new responsibilities, but more than that they see
what they are doing in terms of their Christian discipleship. They

Figure 4.3   A congregation which begins to think

are not just experiencing more busyness and activity as the minister relinquishes hold of all activities, they begin to see what they are doing as having some connection with the faith they are understanding anew through these discussions and through their new responsibilities. Questions like 'What is going in this congregation?' begin to spring up. Even more hopefully, people begin to ask questions about the congregation from the other end. 'What is it for? What are we here for? What is the church for?' In their debates the thinking begins about what it means to be an adult believer today, and what kind of church is needed to support such adult belief, spiritual development and Christian service.

A collective and idealized way of expressing the new experiences like this might be put in the following way: 'As a lay person I am not just a helper in the tasks which the minister has done before, by means of my baptism and confirmation I am called by Christ to serve his people by word and example.'

Figure 4.4 A congregation of shared responsibilities

A congregation of shared responsibilities (Figure 4.4)

One of the most significant developments in the way faith is expressed has come to be in terms of an understanding of the basic commitment made by all in the sacrament of baptism. What has been rediscovered is the experience upon which is built the understanding of our faith. In a parish of shared responsibilities, one way of expressing this sharing is to describe the willingness, and naturalness, of all Christians working together as a discovery of the personal responsibility for ministry which comes through baptism. Each individual responds to the call of God with their talents and with the potential they have for more growth. 'In each one the Holy Spirit reveals His presence, giving something that is for the good of all' (1 Cor 12.7).

Each person in the congregation begins to discover how they can offer themselves for service within the community of faith or in the wider world. They no longer see themselves as the helpers of the minister, or anyone else, but live with the joy of being called by Christ himself to work for the unfolding and realization of the Kingdom wherever they are called to be. Jesus said to the Apostles, 'I no longer call you servants, but friends' (John 15.15).

A congregation which is a community of communities (Figure 4.5)

The congregation is no longer a 'large group' of people but a living community which is being converted more and more into becoming the Body of Christ. Faith and life are shared in human-sized communities. In the discussion groups and in the activity groups, the Word of God becomes the point of departure for Christian living.

The congregation is renewed, forming small Christian communities established as healthy cells. There is a pastoral, priestly role for the minister which far exceeds any concept which could have been dreamed of in the early stages of this development of sharing.

The vocation and mission of lay people

Startling new discoveries have been made. In fact they are both old and new since they embody the essential nature of the communities which became established in the early days of the sharing of the good news of the resurrection of Christ.

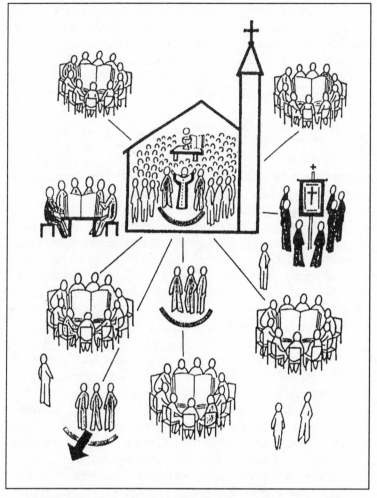

Figure 4.5 A congregation which is a community of communities

- All the baptized, whether lay, religious or pastor, have essentially the same dignity and equality. No one is more 'in the church' than another. What is important is the service or ministry that is accomplished within it.
- First of all we are all brothers and sisters in baptism, then we are set apart by the specific mission to which we are called.
- Everyone is called by their baptism and confirmation to be Christian Apostles: active, evangelical, witnesses to Christ by their words and example.

- Everyone is called to the same 'vocation' of holiness.
- We are all called to live fully human lives as Christ's people.
- The same Gospel guides everyone and makes the same demands. Only the paths are different.
- Everyone shares the same mission: to build or reveal something of the Kingdom of God.

Baptism and vocation

The root of the fundamental, single, Christian vocation is the baptism we have in common, across the denominations, which unites us with Christ as Priest, Prophet and King.

- All the baptized participate directly in the priesthood of Christ: 'You are a chosen race, a kingdom of priests, a consecrated nation, a people of God, chosen to be his and to proclaim his wonders' (1 Peter 2.9). Only the way of participating is different. Sometimes, in some denominations, we speak of the common priesthood of all the baptized and of the ministerial priesthood of the pastors of the church.
- A prophet is someone who speaks in the name of God, inspired by the Gospel. Each true Christian is a prophet, and can and must work jointly in evangelizing primarily through the way in which they choose to order their lives.
- All Christians are called to work for the enlarged realization of the Kingdom of God. This is begun in the family, at work and in the neighbourhood. The imprisonment of the Kingdom is an attempt to restrict the description of God's activity to the ecclesiastical, social and domestic spheres of our lives. Christ the King is Lord of all the world and, as the Good Shepherd, cares for all its people.

The truth in parts

Through such a circumspect look at what a number of writers have produced about collaborative ministry the skeleton of a structure does begin to emerge for us in our time and in each of our situations. We all learn by doing and by examining theories. Different approaches will begin with one or the other. For me, more than anything else, the sense of unity in a common cause, or a harmony in methodology, comes from the assumption that we work from a common set of values and beliefs. Often they are not articulated, sometimes they are more apparent when we or others are seen not to be using collaborative methods. We know that these assumptions are valid and right when we share the joy of seeing those we work with grow and develop, dream new dreams, and take on hitherto unimagined responsibilities.

Collaborative ministry, working as one body, can have a range of interpretations and it can look differently according to local circumstances and denominational approaches. It does, however, have some basic underlying beliefs and requires a commitment on the part of those who work in this way to keep to them. In an inherently hierarchical denomination the work will be hard to put in place. In a denomination or congregation characterized by dependent relationships, many will be confused at first. In clergy-centred congregations tremendous learning will take place as new kinds of growth are experienced. From feeling under-valued and marginalized, clergy will come to see that they can hold the key to personal liberation and tremendous theological dialogue and learning. This concept of communion through community living will be rich food for the faithful and for the searcher.

Notes

1   *Working as One Body* (Church House Publishing, 1995).
2   *The Sign We Give*, Report from the Working Party on Collaborative Ministry, Catholic Bishops' Conference of England and Wales (Matthew James Publishing, 1995).
3   *A Time for Sharing: Collaborative Ministry in Mission*, Board of Mission Occasional Paper no. 6 (Church House Publishing, 1995).
4   See the writings of the Revd Dr George Lovell and Miss Catherine Widdicombe referred to in the Bibliography and also *Varieties of Gifts*, a report of work done in the Diocese of Bradford 1994–97. Available from The Diocesan Secretary, Cathedral Hall, Stott Hill, Bradford BD1 4ET.

5

Understanding Clergy

How do clergy understand themselves? Fortunately, we do not have to give our undivided attention to this question. What concerns us is the relationship between 'lay' people and those who are ordained. Those outside the churches in our everyday communities also have a view about who clergy are and how they fit into the life of a local community.

A number of things about the clergy are certain. Their position in society has changed. For a number of centuries in some northern European countries Roman Catholic clergy have had little or no place in the wider community. Reasons for this are both to do with the history of Roman Catholicism and also because the Catholic communities in many countries were made up of migrants whose priests were very much chaplains to those gathered groups. Similarly, Protestant clergy in other European countries have suffered persecution. Free Church ministers enjoyed being 'non-conformists' and, with their congregations, used that position to make a particular contribution to a local community. Anglicans have probably suffered from having their clergy closely linked with particular strata and social groups in English society. One of the disorientations they have suffered is the loss of status and privilege on the part of those 'feeder' groups. Anglican clergy now come from a wide cross-section of society. In doing so they bring a new richness to their ranks. They also suffer from hesitancy and confusion about their relationship with the society from which they were drawn.

This history together with tremendous changes in developed Western society have placed those who are ordained in a quite different position in relation to those among whom they live and work. Professor Roy Niblett has written most tellingly in the journal *Crucible* about this when reflecting on what will be the

even more changed position of clergy in twenty-first-century
Europe.[1] He talks about the ways in which the effectiveness of
clergy is lessened by the constant stress under which they have
to do their jobs. They not only have the pressure of overwork in
their congregations, they minister in communities where crime
may be high, drug abuse prevalent and the breakdown of marriage and family life a daily pastoral occurrence. They will be
working in areas where, while having the same social expectations, their income will be considerably lower than most in their
communities. They will be expected to work longer hours, can
afford fewer holidays and look forward to a much later retirement age than is becoming common among professional
workers.

Just as seriously, Niblett points out, is the new way in which
clergy are having to come to terms with their own difficulties over
the public affirmation of orthodox belief. He says that avoidance, conservatism or commitment to social action are ways in
which clergy learn to survive:

> Repeat the words said to be necessary but put your heart
> into the tasks around you, which goodness knows are
> hard enough, challenging enough, absorbing enough.
> Alternatively one can follow and concentrate loyally
> upon traditions which, after all, have for hundreds of
> years served both church and community well. Such loy-
> alty should overpower doubts – are they not temptations
> under another name?

I can understand and sympathize with clergy who think and
live in these ways. However, for our study it is important to
say that many people are not as confused as is often thought
about the place of the minister in a congregation. That is also
true of many non-churchgoers who ask particular things of
clergy in a community. I am convinced that there are mental
models about types of minister, and these are held very deeply
in the consciousness of many people. I want to set out what
some of these types are. In doing so I will try to reflect
strongly-held perspectives from congregations and local communities as well as preferences expressed by ministers. These
may look like caricatures or they may make connections
with how clergy work from their strengths, as well as

going some way to explain how they compensate for their weaknesses.

Before I begin a description of these ministerial types I do want to acknowledge that confusion and uncertainty are very real feelings in the lives of many ministers and lay people. Much of this uncertainty arises from a mismatch between expectations of a particular model or concept of minister and the way in which the role is carried out. When people expect or hope for one thing and get another they feel confused or let down. When clergy are expected to perform in a particular role or way but see themselves as a very different type of minister, they feel restricted or misunderstood. Collusion with an inappropriate set of expectations brings feelings of dishonesty or a lack of integrity. A refusal to work in particular ways may confuse those whose expectations are very different or may leave a gap in a community where a different person has previously been happy with a different role.

There is a new ecclesiastical library of books about how the clergy are confused and about how they are trying to redefine their roles. Each denomination can have their own book-stack! Robin Greenwood has written in a theological and searching way about understandings and attempts at redefinition in *Transforming Priesthood*.[2] His own introduction sets out the confusion felt by lay people and clergy, from many denominations.

> I observe considerable bewilderment and anger among clergy at the changes in the Church, and a parallel lack of courage and confidence on the part of those laity who are eager to be stretched in their knowledge of God, and to bring about a new way of being church. Clergy often express a conviction that they feel redundant because the laity have somehow taken their place. Others have gladly given assent with their heads to the vital role of the laity in the Church, yet are held back emotionally from sharing the power which inherited patterns left in their hands. Equally, there are laity who feel rejected because, despite constant reference to collaborative ministry as an idea, the patterns of their church's life still do not give them 'permission' to be treated as of equal value to the clergy.

With these sentiments as a starting-off point, let us begin to look at the 'models' of ministry which I see in the minds and lives of many congregations and of the clergy who serve them.

Basic beliefs

By 'model' I mean the often unexpressed basic beliefs by which the clergy will try to set out their lives. Some, in a rather whimsical way, can be read by the way in which they dress. The Diocesan Secretary of a former diocese in which I worked had a cartoon showing all the humour of how clergy used to look. One was always called 'Father'. He would wear a black suit, often be in a cassock in the street, and have a strong idea of himself as a priest with a strong public persona. Another figure in the cartoon had on a tweed sports jacket, wore grey flannel trousers and smoked a pipe. We could add now to that picture the clergy person in a loose-fitting pullover, jeans or corduroy trousers, hardly ever with a clerical collar being worn. Another might be happier working with a computer than by the sick bed. Following the advent of committee membership as a perceived route to the 'top' in our denominations we can have another person neatly in a relatively expensive suit, files in hand, going at quite a pace from one meeting to the next. Probably a mobile phone will keep a tenuous contact with the parish for urgent messages and necessary calls.

More seriously, there are real perceptions which clergy and laity will recognize in these descriptions. They are neither bad or good. They become difficult when the person is trapped in that role, or when their public profile is used as a shield behind which to hide. I want to set out here some of the healthy and very good images or models of clergy which enrich our experience of the ordained. Without the human beings behind these public faces all concepts of ordained ministry would be reduced to the role of a mere public functionary. Remember also the very old joke, that for recruits to the clergy, all we have to draw on are the members of the laity.

The pastor as shepherd

Congregations and local communities have a picture of the local minister as someone who visits them at home, calls personally on anyone who is known to be ill and who is always willing to give a welcome in their own home to those who call.

Where do these perceptions come from? Quite clearly some of the ideas come from the Bible. King David was a good shepherd boy who always cared for and defended his flock. The prophet Isaiah used the image of a lamb suffering for the sins of many. It seems that Jesus used some of this imagery in describing his understanding of his own life. St John described Jesus as the Good Shepherd.

In our communities the priest, vicar or minister is expected to be like the good shepherd who knows the sheep and is known by them. The lost are searched out and brought home amid rejoicing. The sheep know the voice of the shepherd and respond to his call. It is a picture of trust, of care and of dependency. The pastoral image of shepherd and the life of self-sacrifice modelled on Christ become intertwined as an ideal way of life.

If a part of this concept is not lived out by a minister, there will be general disappointment. When ministers feel that they cannot fulfil all the expectations placed upon them, they experience a sense of disappointment and frustration. Health, family life, free time and personal friendships may begin to suffer. Lay people are reluctant to take on pastoral work if they see that their own minister does not give a high value to this work. Not many lay people will have heard of George Herbert other than as a metaphysical poet or hymn-writer. Many pastoral clergy will have taken their model from Herbert's description of the conscientious, visiting, praying parson in his influential *A Priest to the Temple*, written in the few years from 1630 to 1633 when he was Vicar of Bemerton near Salisbury. Herbert's contribution to this pastoral tradition is explored very well by Anthony Russell in *The Country Parson*, one of his series of books on the evolution of clerical life.[3]

The Curé d'Ars

An acceptable variation on the pastoral model is that which gives great emphasis to spirituality, guidance and counselling. My description of this type of ministry, in its modern form, comes from Jean-Baptiste Marie Vianney. He was the local priest at Ars in France from 1818 until his death in 1859. The ministry he developed was one where people travelled great distances to seek his wise counsel. It was said that towards the end of his life he spent from sixteen to eighteen hours a day in the confessional! The contemporary equivalent will not do this but will see the task as being very people-centred. Time will be given to developing expertise in spiritual guidance, and individuals will be given much time and attention. A variation on this will be the person who develops skills in pastoral counselling or psychotherapy.

The Curé d'Ars minister just may be a person who is likely to be lax or not give a high priority to paperwork. They may be relatively unable to oganize themselves or their parish. Others may have to take on even routine tasks. It will be a fine line between this role being one of genuine care for many people or an avoidance of the basic parish pump tasks expected of the responsible minister. Laity will have to be very discerning about whether to affirm such a priest in that ministry or to encourage them out into a more balanced life. A church obsessed with fund-raising, numbers and the maintenance of buildings cannot afford many such people in sole charge of a congregation and its plant. Their value for the future may lie in being a resource within a team, though teamwork almost certainly will not be the principal characteristic of a Curé d'Ars!

The social activist

Congregations do not always figure highly in the minister's perception of how a life is lived. There are those who see the main thrust of the Gospel as being out into the community or into the world. The Gospel is understood as being about the changing of social conditions, the righting of wrongs and the changing of oppressive structures. In this century Charles Gore and Archbishop William Temple have brought this type of ministry into prominence. The years from Cardinal Manning to Archbishop Worlock have seen a close identification of Catholic leaders with social questions. There has hardly been a President of the Methodist Conference who has not addressed major public issues.

Again, the ministry of Jesus is a model. He chose to eat and spend time with tax collectors and sinners. He told the disciples that when they visited the prisoner, the bereaved, or those in any kind of trouble, they visited him. Even more strongly, the lives of the prophets of the Old Testament show a concern of righteous indignation for abuses of power.

Many clergy have chosen to take up the model of social concern as a main platform for their ministries. In the local church there are significant contributions being made to local community life and care by such people. The balance between a ministry to the community and that of maintaining and nurturing a congregation is a difficult one to maintain. Congregations can feel neglected – or that the role of their minister is to support and equip lay people for their lives at work and in the community, and not to be overactive in these tasks themselves. The minister who is not seen to be showing an interest in the problems of a local community will be perceived as having an imbalance in their understanding of a care beyond that of the church gates.

The evangelist

As something of a contrast to the social activist, the evangelist will place great emphasis on the congregation and on bringing people into it. Concerns for social ministries and involvement in the wider life of the community or denomination will be less prominent. The model for these clergy will be John the Baptist as well as the uncompromising sayings of Jesus, or of the early believers. A direct message will be presented which offers a choice to turn and become a committed believer. Such a model is gaining in prominence in the denominations.

Many will say the time of the evangelist has come. Decline in church attendance and in residual belief has brought the need for a period when religion and Christian belief have a much more distinctive stance of their own. On occasions an evangelical ministry will stand over-against the world, though this is by no means always the case. There can be no doubt that unless the developed world is to take the path leading towards Bonhoeffer's 'religionless Christianity' there has to be an emphasis placed by the denominations on re-establishing a confidence in their traditions, in communicating their beliefs and in giving a contemporary liturgical expression of them to a wider public.

No longer can basic Christian belief be assumed of a great majority in the Western world. Enquirers into the faith will need a clear and relatively straightforward presentation if they are to grasp the basic story. Dangers in too much of a 'tell' or hard-sell approach are that a person's religious search up to that point is not valued. Past experiences have to be disregarded ready to take on a new life within the community of believers. Congregations with an emphasis on conversions and in drawing newcomers in, on occasions find it difficult to accept that new Christians will continue to grow in their faith and will need a broader nurturing than that of repetition of the same gospel emphases.

The organizer

A necessary feature of the life of any congregation is that it should not only have good pastoral care but also that it should be effectively led and managed. Such a model of minister cuts across the ideal which many have when they consider their calling. Indeed younger clergy and ordinands have said to me that they do not relish the prospect of coming into full-time work in a denomination which will expect these roles of them.

On the other hand many ministers are fulfilled by knowing that their congregation is cared for by an effective organization, where responsibilities are clear and tasks well described. There is a good case to be made out that pastoral care is not carried out effectively unless administration is done well. The good pastor is the good organizer.

Problems come when the balance becomes tilted. Congregations can feel overorganized. There can be too many rotas and lists. A too-busy congregation can take up every minute of free time. Congregation members can fear the minister coming up to them or coming to visit because it will mean that they are going to be asked to take on another job.

A local congregation has to run smoothly. People do need to be clear about what is being asked of them. Everyone needs to know what the overall aims of the congregation are. There is a responsibility to raise money and to manage buildings well. Parish clubs, groups and activities do need to be organized. The skill of the organizer minister is in having the right touch so that congregation members will offer their services with enthusiasm but at the same time have the complete freedom to be able to say 'No'.

The bureaucrat

There are clergy who enjoy sitting on committees. This province is not exclusive to them and many lay people have been drawn into the same ecclesiastical superstructure. Free Churches are founded on the concept that lay people have principal, or equal, control of the life of a local congregation. From the advent of lay participation in Church of England congregations when Parochial Church Councils were established in 1922, to the full flowering of Synodical Government in 1970, there has been ample opportunity for committee life to flourish. The radical proposals of the Turnbull Report in 1995 may clip this to some extent and move the Church of England towards a more executive style of government. At the same time the Roman Catholic Church is in a slow process of development from a narrow executive to more devolved ways.

This particular form of life has suited, or even encouraged, ministers who want the church to be participative and to see this come about through a local government, civil service committee model. The particular problem experienced by many has been a slowing down or even halting of decision-making processes. Equally, synodical government has encouraged a 'party' type of polarizing in church life. This is a world away from the intentions of the original architects whose aim was to encourage clergy and lay participation and to develop a greater sense of accountability and shared responsibility.

There are now clergy who live out a model of government for churches in this way. What has to be questioned is a view of church which encourages this thought. The Gospel has rarely been proclaimed through the working of committees, and clergy who engage in such activities have to balance their time with the varied demands which are made on them in the full round of their duties.

Equally, there is the question of who is being encouraged into the churches and the picture which they are given. Christianity has first of all to be about living a full life of service in the world, supported and nurtured by a vital congregation. Conversion is not to committees and to salvation by resolutions and amendments. The role of the ecclesiastical bureaucrat is necessary and fulfilling when it is placed in the context of service and is fired by the burning desire to bring about change and to get things done.

Less than full-time in the parish

Not all clergy work out their roles in full-time parochial ministry. A recent and sometimes disturbing characteristic of the practice of stipendiary ministers in our churches is that, rather than a minister having one or more churches, they may have more than one job given to them by their denomination. Collaborative work becomes essential in these circumstances. Such 'other' jobs often come in the form of a specialist ministry of some kind, industrial chaplain, hospital chaplain, agricultural chaplain, youth chaplain or another kind of denominational specialist. Such appointments can take a minister away from the local pastoral situation for a few hours or for several days in a week. The absence of finance, or the will by some denominations, to provide full-time specialists more often than ever now means that such appointments are called part-time or 'dual role' and are linked with a congregational appointment.

Dual-role ministers

It is important here that we take time to look at this different situation. Dual-role ministers have two, or more, designated areas of work – two types of focus for their work. Usually they also work on two different physical pieces of territory. This can lead to a split-personality kind of lifestyle where different behaviour is left behind or adopted as one moves from one sector to another. The very title 'dual role' suggests, gives permission for, different roles to be acted out. There need not be anything intrinsically wrong with this. It may well be the only way that some ministers can work.

'All ministry is multi-role' says Malcolm Foy in *Twofold*, the dual-role ministers' newsletter for autumn 1995. Those clergy who have sole parochial charge or full-time specialist posts know that this is true. Part of the expertise of the ordained person is to learn how to move, and to change mood, approach and style almost completely from one pastoral visit to another. I can remember doing some appraisal training for a diocese where people were asked to write a five-line biography of themselves so that they might be matched well in a peer appraisal system. One wrote that after twenty years in ministry he was now getting used to working with the 'feel quaint factor' in many of his ministerial contacts.

One ministry

The writings of very many dual-role ministers emphasize time and time again that they do not see themselves as having two

Christian ministries but one call which is being worked out in two different situations. Oneness is important. It counters immediately the schizophrenic connotations of 'dual' in dual-role ministries. It also forces us to address the question of oneness in debates about stipendiary and non-stipendiary, specialist and beneficed, ministers in secular employment and ordained members of local ministry teams. The 'one' in all this is the one ministry which all the people of God share through their baptism, and the oneness which we all share is the calling which we have, from God and the church, to the order of the ordained within our church and denomination.

Two jobs

The difference is then that dual-role ministers have two jobs, and working relationships become an issue. Two jobs, probably one with responsibility for a congregation, and one a specialist-sector piece of work. Each has a different discipline and each makes a different set of demands. The different disciplines mean that it is better to have something about both written down. That in itself will pose a new challenge. Two jobs also means two sets of expectations, three if private lives and families are included. It is essential that there is a job description for each part of the job and that both parties see both parts of the description. Regular reviews need to be put in place at the outset both for the working out of the job and for the integrated process of reflective practice required of the minister.

Horror stories

At an early stage in any reflection of split appointments there needs to be a recitation of the problems which often occur, some of which may be avoided. I have been involved in putting together many such appointments both in industrial mission and in adult education. Bishops and pastoral committees (in the Church of England) see a difficult, run-down, unpastoral-reorganizable parish as ripe for a dual-role appointment. This is to be resisted unless it is seen to be sensible for some other reason.

Difficult parishes require more work not less. It simply builds up the stress if a minister returns from the sector part of the job to an uphill task and a pile of problems which, because they are immediate and identifiable, can easily dominate a day and a week. Specialist work can be squeezed out because here you have to make your own running.

No one expects to see you. Diaries have to be filled in with the running you want to make, the visits you will do, otherwise empty spaces will be gobbled up by what is seen as equally, or more tangible, parish business.

There is a problem here for partners and families who are placed in difficult parishes. They do not necessarily go away to another environment. The pressures of living can be great, either in an urban area stacked with social problems or a remote rural village with cautious natives or incomers who use the village as a dormitory and who want more, not less, of the nostalgic rural idyll. Working relationships are really at the heart of dual-role ministries. They have to be worked at. The right establishment can be very draining – and extremely time-consuming.

Working relationships

The key to success in dual-role appointments, as in all other work, is the establishment of good working relationships. I am sure that the success possible in developing this area lies in regular evaluation. It begins with a clear contract for both sides of the job. It means that 'someone' will have negotiated the appointment with both sides, and that they will even have spoken together. Who is this someone? Occasionally, it will be a system for appointments in a denomination which will name the responsible person. Sometimes you will have to set up the process yourselves. The recipe for disaster is the part of our ecclesiastical culture which either panders to the 'talented individual' model where the minister has sole responsibility to work it out for themselves, or the *laissez-faire* model where it is all too disturbing to actually discuss what needs to be done. 'It will all work out.' If it goes well the denomination takes the credit. If it goes wrong then the minister was not up to it! Agreements at the outset, then, make it possible for regular evaluations to take place. These can be conducted at a number of levels. I favour a short check-out after three months and a revision of job descriptions, if necessary, after one year. It is at this length of time that unexpressed expectations begin to reveal themselves and conflict is emerging. If an appointment is for five years, then there needs to be a major review after four years.

I was fortunate enough to be invited to share in the conference of the national network for dual-role ministers in 1995. Many of their achievements could be celebrated and even more of their frustrations aired. Many felt that they were at the point where denominations had made a compromise and put two large jobs together in difficult-to-manage halves. Many rejoiced at having the stimulation of a parish and a specialist post. I was able to set out, with the aid of a diagram (Figure 5.1), how the work might be inter-related, how one theological understanding is connected to the other and how their work contributes to spiritual growth and understanding.

Where is the ordained ministry going?

In looking at the outworking of clerical ministry and going on this excursion into dual-role appointments, we are brought to see something of the changing nature of the expectations placed on ordained ministers and how these expectations relate to new relationships with lay people and with congregations. The position of those in ordained ministry has changed already. Worker and non-stipendiary ministers have been saying that to the church for at least thirty years now. It is sector ministers who can make profound theological reflections as well as give practical advice on this new but established feature of practice within the ordained ministry. They have more experience in this than anyone else. Equally, they are the unheard group within the ranks of the ordained. They are neither fully committed parish ministers nor totally absorbed specialist or worker priests. Chapter meetings and Fraternals are hard to find time for. Synods are irrelevant unless you are the speaker. Yet clergy with licences, those with dual-role jobs, those in secular employment and those in house-for-duty posts make up a significant part of the ordained people within our denominations. Their presence already reflects a changed church. But many of us carry on as if there is the 'real' ministry of those in stipendiary posts and those others who are there where they are because they have some kind of a problem or they are not fully committed. Do they really need to be ordained to do the specialist work they are engaged in? Nigel Peyton has written about this real situation in a very descriptive way in *Ministry* with an article called 'Two for the price of one?' He ends with a sobering sentence: 'Two for the

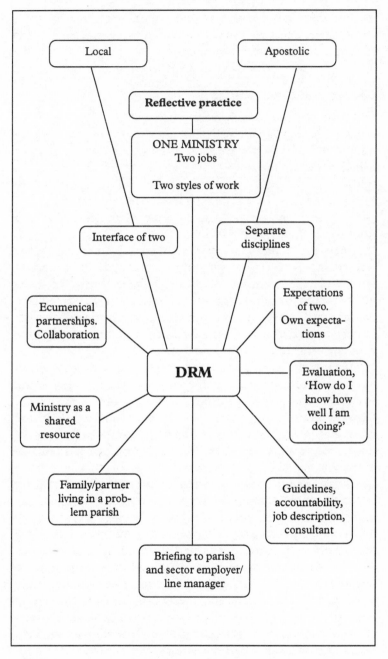

Figure 5.1 'All ministry is multi-role': working relationships in dual-role ministry

price of one may not always turn out to be the bargain it appears, and for every success story an unhappy price may be paid by ministers and ministries elsewhere.'[4]

Clergy and local ministry

From all that has already been discussed about collaborative ministry, how clergy are seen and how they see themselves, it is natural to move to a discussion of local ministry. Across our principal denominations a change is taking place from the more traditional, clerically based professional full-time stipendiary ministry towards a way of understanding the local church and its congregation which expects its lay members to recognize and want to use their varied gifts in the service of God through giving their time and 'ministries' to their local church. A key element in this developing situation is that clergy and laity *together* are becoming committed to working together on the many tasks, prayer, worship, education, pastoral care, evangelism, preparation for baptism or confirmation which characterize the life of the local church, many of which would previously have been the province of the minister.

What is the exact understanding of this new concept which has been developed and which is called local ministry? Central to our theme, Robin Greenwood, who has written in most helpful ways on this subject says: 'Local can be summarized in two ways. First it is a unit that is able to sustain and work with a visible team of people. Second it is the scale on which it is possible for people to relate person to person.'[5]

If that is a little too abstract and impersonal, local ministry is developed in a number of Anglican dioceses and has a much more familiar face. In such places, either one parish or in a group of parishes, lay people are called out by their local congregations to perform certain pastoral, priestly and organizational tasks. The diocese or other Christian unit agrees to take a part in the selection of such local ministers and to provide support and training. In some dioceses members of the local ministry group call out one person to be ordained as a priest to exercise a ministry only within that particular group of parishes and called a Local Non-Stipendiary Minister (LNSM).

What is important and a key development for the future is the constitution and make-up of local ministry teams. What is

most interesting is that it is not just those involved who are commissioned in this local ministry: it is the whole congregation.
Everyone shares in the commission and in the work which is
being done. Local ministry is in the most definite sense both
shared and *collaborative*. The concept of ordained and lay choosing to work together in new and innovative ways is integral to this
work. Undoubtedly it demands both trust and confidence in one
another from all involved. It certainly reflects an excitement
about a vision of what can be achieved in a local community
through this new kind of partnership.

Non-stipendiary clergy

In addition to the relationships which clergy have with congregations, there are now significant numbers of clergy who do not
see the main focus of their work as related to a local parish congregation at all. They will see their ministry as an ordained
person in their place of work. The contribution which these clergy are making to our new understanding of the nature of the
church in the world is tremendous and is being well explored in
some exciting studies. Our present task is to look at the way in
which clergy are related to congregations, so a look at this work
falls outside our declared sphere of exploration.

Clergy who do this kind of work are also members of congregations. They need to be understood and to be given support
for what they are doing, which is often in positions where their
faith is exposed and under constant scrutiny. Parish clergy and
congregations often make the mistake, for which they can be forgiven, of valuing these NSM work-focused clergy for what they
can contribute to parish life in their spare time rather than valuing them for what they give in their secular work. Work-focused
NSMs will appreciate the fact that their ministry is recognized if
they are included in the membership of the local parish team,
though daytime meetings which are easier for the stipendiary
clergy will be a difficulty.

Other NSMs see themselves as parish-based. Some are there
in their 'spare' time after work, others give generously of their time
through the week and only receive their working expenses. The
danger of exploitation of such people is great. Their contribution
to the life of the local church is becoming increasingly significant.
As with dual-role ministers, it is essential that they have a contract

or agreement, about how much they will contribute to a local church. If this is done then at least there is discussion and understanding on both sides about what is expected.

House-for-duty appointments

An even newer phenomenon is for NSM clergy or retired clergy to live, rent free, in the vicarage in exchange for some days duty in the parish and the taking of Sunday services. Experience is showing that these appointments work best if the congregation also has the oversight of a stipendiary minister who will have overall charge of more than one parish, with the NSM, house-for-duty, acting as assistant in and residing in a different parish. Once again, contracts and written agreements are essential if misunderstandings are to be kept to a minimum. An NSM who stimulates and contributes to the life of a local ministry team will be a valued asset. Often, through present or previous secular employment, they will be more familiar with team and collaborative working methods than some 'sole charge' clergy.

Experience assessed

Local ministry projects have been at work in sufficient numbers for a first stocktaking to be done. In 1994 the Edward King Institute for Ministry Development held a consultation for those involved in local ministry teams. A tremendous amount of experience and wisdom emerged from this meeting of the converted.[6] Two fundamental and commonly-held beliefs were acknowledged and shared by those present:

- The belief that through baptism God calls each person to ministry.
- The belief that God gives to the church the gifts that it needs to be the church in a particular place.

The process of meeting to exchange good practice and reflect upon the work being done proved to be an exciting and supportive experience. Many there spoke of the excitement of engaging in the work and of the joy of being trusted and valued by their local churches. Of course, the greatest benefit was in what those congregations had to offer to their local communities. Here were, and are, groups of people trained and authorized to extend the love of God through special tasks and roles into their local communities. Work is organized, supported and evaluated. Ministry teams do not create an 'elite' who have superior positions in a congregation. They are a recognition of the ways in which the already present skills and abilities within the members of a congregation can be harnessed and focused in ways that can bring a greater effectiveness to what a local church is trying to do. They are an acting out of what is seen as a new call from God for our time.

Focus on the invisible

One of the consequences of a strong understanding of one view of priesthood and one model of church is that the others tend to become invisible. When very strong views are held and a life is aimed at achieving certain clearly defined roles then other interpretations are either dismissed or brushed aside, or are simply not seen at all.

Another characteristic of a strongly owned version either of church or of ministry is that it is understood as the *mature* view. Once others have been a little longer in the faith then, it is thought, they will grow up a little more and see that 'we' have something more. There is a particular challenge to evangelicalism in this view. What does a mature evangelicalism look like? Many people come to faith through a converting series of events. Often now with little previous knowledge of the faith they have a great desire both for certainty and to know more. They need what a strongly biblical faith can offer them. Many congregations of this nature come to feel themselves to be transit camps. New members come in a steady flow but an equal number seem to leave because they are looking for something more.

Focusing on the invisible asks churches to examine what they are not providing and to attempt to value beliefs and practices once dismissed as 'not the way we do things here'. Growing churches need enthusiasm born of a strong vision and a set of what are seen as certainties. Churches which will continue to grow will respect and learn to value what feeds and inspires others. Focusing on the invisible reduces rivalry and allows for comprehensiveness within a still clearly defined tradition.

The Holy Trinity, ecumenism and reciprocal ministries

Interestingly, the Catholic Bishops in *The Sign We Give* use the idea of communion to describe our earthly relationships as well as our spiritual contact with God in the Eucharist. The French Dominican Yves Congar, who was one of the pioneers of Catholic involvement in ecumenical questions, reflects the same approach to community and communion. His thinking is well described by Christopher Meakin, an Anglican/Lutheran priest and theologian working in Sweden: '. . . the Trinity is not just the theological and ontological cause of ecclesial communion, but should be the exemplary cause and model of the human structuring of that reality. . .'[7] Meakin goes on to comment that the lack of understanding between the different parts of the church about being parts of one mutual communion has led it to go on and supplant this mutuality in communion by a pyramidal conception of church.

This inherited understanding of hierarchy has made those who would prefer to work with a revised theological understanding of the structures of the church ask serious questions about collaborative participation in a hierarchical organization. Such a professionally structured pyramid of the internally 'employed' has made integration into the life of a church difficult for non-stipendiary and dual-role ministers and produced illusory barriers to belief in collaborative working practices.

Changed leadership styles

The new task of the clergyman or woman as leader is to make collegiality of activity possible within those engaged in the life of a congregation and then of those within the ministry team. In 1968 Cardinal Suenens wrote: 'A true leader will find his place when he has succeeded in helping others to find theirs.' That remark could be the motto or benchmark for clergy who are committed to this way of working. The practice of ministry for the future will be *collaborative*, it will be *varied* in the ways in which those who are ordained are understood and used, and it will be *local* in the ways in which clergy and lay people – often across denominations – commit themselves not to do separately anything that they could and should do together.

It is often helpful to be able to move from what seems to be the intractably difficult to a more lighthearted view of how ministers are perceived. What I have added below is attributed to W. Edward Harris and was first seen in a publication of the Unitarian Universalist Ministers Association in the United States. I adapted this English version while I edited the journal *Ministry*.

Real ministers	• are never late;
	• don't use answering machines;
	• don't lead Holy Land tours;
	• remember everyone's names;
	• have read every book in their libraries;
	• aren't afraid to take on the mother of the bride;
	• have children by immaculate conception;
	• churches are always growing;
	• never split churches;
	• don't read denominational mailings;
	• know who is ill and who is in hospital;
	• don't do funerals on their day off;
	• stand up to organists;
	• are never the last to leave the church;
	• don't know where the vacuum cleaner is kept;
	• don't need to write out their sermons;
	• know when to stop;
	• don't edit their parish magazines;
	• always wear black clerical shirts;
	• never get involved in parish arguments;
	• have perfect marriages and ideal children;
	• make everyone happy;
	• never worry about their sermons;
	• never worry about any of the above.

Notes

1   Roy Niblett, 'Churches in twenty-first century Britain', *Crucible* (July–September 1997).
2   Robin Greenwood, *Transforming Priesthood* (SPCK, 1995), p. 2.
3   Anthony Russell, *The Country Parson* (SPCK, 1993).
4   Nigel Peyton, 'Two for the price of one', *Ministry*, edition 27 (Winter 1996). *Ministry* is the journal of the Edward King Institute for Ministry Development, MODEM and The Adult Catechumenate Network and can be obtained from Mrs V. Tyler, Church House, Churchyard, Hitchin, Herts SG5 1HP.
5   Greenwood, *op. cit.*
6   *Ministry*, Local Ministry conference report, edition 24 (Winter 1994).
7   Christopher Meakin, *'The Same but Different?': The Relationship Between Unity and Diversity in the Theological Ecumenism of Yves Congar* (Studia Theologica Lundensia 50, Lund University Press, 1995), p. 73.

6

Understanding Relationships

There was a time when 'going to church' meant just that. In the Middle Ages villagers or townspeople attended the Mass and most probably just stood in church while the priest performed the service, with his back to the people, behind a rood screen. They were called to give attention to the most sacred parts by the ringing of bells. There was a sense of community here insofar as villagers could stand around and talk when their attentions or devotions were not required. The more pious could read the wall paintings. In the churches of the Reformation, sitting and attending to the preacher was important. Pews were set out in rows, and attention to a point of focus was required. The personal faith between a believer and God was what became most important, a private faith for increasingly private people. For the separateness of family life and to contain children, box pews were constructed in many churches. Movement between members of a congregation – and the idea that they would sit in different places each Sunday – was not contemplated.

How different things have become in almost all congregations today. Almost as a reaction to the loss of community in many societies, but also showing rediscoveries in liturgical practice, worship has become an event in which many members of a congregation participate. 'Lay' people share in the readings and the prayers. There has been something of a return to earlier times, with groups of musicians leading or taking part in worship. In addition, the sharing of the Kiss of Peace by handshakes or 'hugs' has broken down the inhibitions of some for whom human contact in church was previously reserved for a handshake with the vicar at the church door – if it could not absolutely be avoided. The sum total of all this is that congregation members are much more aware of each other than they have ever been before. There is a deliberate meeting for what is too easily called 'fellowship'. The life of small groups within congregations means that, in homes or church rooms, believers and enquirers share their personal hopes and the intimacies of their lives with one another, often at a quite deep level. This is usually done with a great amount of professionalism. Groups are well led and members are aware of the boundaries for themselves in any discussion and sharing. However, a relaxed atmosphere can easily appear to give permission for less than appropriate behaviour. Many congregation members have had their friendliness or genuine empathy mistaken for something else.

People have become congregations

The liturgical movement has made us aware of one another in church. In many places the priest or minister now 'presides' over the Eucharist, faces us, and we have a strong sense of meeting one another as well as God in worship. The active life of a congregation is made up of the use of willing voluntary time from its members. The priest or minister has a much greater desire to become alongside the people. Christian names are used for clergy in a way unthought-of a century ago. Clergy too can have their genuine pastoral intentions misunderstood. In all these human interactions there is an element in which we are meeting our own unexpressed needs as well as offering care and support to others.

I regard these changes in the participative nature of congregational life as good. They emphasize the communal nature of the Christian life and, when done effectively, provide a model for how people and groups might operate in their wider society. Leadership is shared and now, in most denominations, it is shared between men and women.

In the Christian intention to care and to get close to those in need, as with all good things, there is another side. Relationships do break down. The good intentions of Christian friendship do get misunderstood. None of us completely knows how our motives are received by others. Quite certainly there are those who come to church for companionship and who use membership of groups to meet some of their basic human needs for socializing and much more. In the true spirit of this Christian gospel, the church should and does exist for the broken, the poor, the bereaved and the lonely, though the strong do not have anything of a monopoly on security, and need to come in also. The congregation is also a place where women and men meet together in sets of relationships outside family or work. One of the sadnesses of life in many congregations is that husbands and wives do not share together in churchgoing. The congregation is not a 'club', but single people and those without their partners do come together in this different situation to learn more about their faith. In this atmosphere of supportive fellowship a new question comes to the surface and has to be acknowledged and explored. How can friendships be made and sustained within a congregation?

Newly-defined relationships

If the possibility of 'starting at the other end' were allowed with the question of personal relationships between adults and children, men and men, women and women, and women and men in churches, it might be that we would ask 'What would it be like if . . . friendships were defined not by the role which people have, but by the working relationships which they are able to establish with one another?'

Friendship and role

Friendships demand equality. For a truly deep and mutually refreshing relationship to be able to develop there has to be an authentic meeting of those willing to share hopes, dreams and vulnerability with one another. Is this possible within congregations and between men and women in leadership roles in the churches?

In a good phrase from the Alban Institute's Celia Hahn, 'Friendship inhabits a special territory in the human heart. Here, as in no other human bond, we stand in a graced space marked by the paradox of intimacy and open freedom, a haven from cramped family quarters and from the vast, uncaring world.'[1] It is in this 'graced space' in our congregational relationships, given to us by God, that we have the special privilege of coming close to other people in a way that is only open to us through the faith we share together. This privileged sharing, of course, brings with it the responsibility of remembering that we would not have the opportunities but for the tradition of acting responsibly established by others.

Most of us have a natural desire to come close to other people. We form friendships for just this purpose. Are there differences between men and women in their desire for intimacy? In stereotyped caricatures it is said of the personality types of many men that they prefer 'distance and doing'. Male career ladders do not have room for too many people on the same rung. Many men do not know anyone very well except their partners.

There are stereotypes for women also. Sometimes it is said that friendships are more important to them than many would admit. Women find closeness and confidantes in their friendships. In working relationships it is not conventionally easy for men and women to be friends, though some great research and business partnerships are indeed between exceptional men and women. The stereotypes say that men are strong on loyalty, they will stand side by side in a common cause, but will hardly be close friends on the sports field or in the pub. Such statements provoke ridicule, and rightly so. But there is truth in mockery as in humour. We do need to understand ourselves, and admit our feminine and masculine parts if we are ever to grow in wholeness.

Friendship requires the kind of reciprocal relationship which, when it works well between women and women, men and men or women and men, is precious. It has as its foundation a willingness to accept equality between two persons and requires a delicate language in description or it evaporates by being named and described at all.

Wendy Wright, also writing for the Alban Institute,[2] comes close to poetry and certainly goes beyond much of our natural reserve. She speaks of the creative intimacy of friendship between women and men as something which is 'poised delicately in that role which is neither lover nor stranger' and she says the intimacy of such relationships is 'not becoming either a union of lovers or a marriage or – retreating into the cool and safely negotiated corridors of an acquaintance'.

Christian friendship

Asking for friendship involves risk. We do not know if we shall be accepted or whether our needs and motives will be misunderstood. Jesus can be a model, an example here. While many think that closeness to Jesus can only be achieved in the privacy of their own prayers or spirituality, a reading of the Gospels gives a different message. With both male and female friends, Jesus seems to be able to move easily between mutual self-revelation and companionship in action. In Luke's intimate picture of the woman washing Jesus' feet with her tears and hair we see the portrait of a warm friend (Mary Magdalene?) who accepted emotional and physical closeness with comfort. The intimacy of Jesus' friendships with men is evident in his crying over the death of his friend Lazarus and in his lying right up against the Beloved Disciple at supper. The shy, bleeding, woman's surreptitious touch is met by an instant and empathic understanding of her need.

Companionship

Sally McFague[3] says: 'Jesus is a parable of God's friendship with us at the most profound level.' If we think about the actions of Jesus and his very person as a parable, we have opened up to us a picture of the Holy One who travels with us and who remains with us in our adventures and troubles. The metaphor of 'companion' (one who breaks bread with us) also holds in tension the concerns about friendship as being or doing. It is wonderful and reassuringly safe to rehabilitate the seemingly quaint Victorian concept of companion. It can carry this delightful dimension of Jesus' friendship with us and suggest the right kinds of friendship which we can make with one another.

Such a development of these concepts of friendship and intimacy go some way to explain traditional visiting patterns of clergy. There are high expectations that the 'clergy will call' without the fulfilment of which no amount of lay visiting can be authenticated. This illustration from a Catholic priest expresses the relationship well,

'People are always dropping in to see "if you've got a minute Father". Catholics don't usually make an appointment with their parish priest, as they would with the dentist or solicitor. At first this seemed odd to me after some years in the business world. But then I realized that they don't think of the priest as a professional, but as their friend, and it's OK to drop in on a friend.' Such visiting is made more difficult today with the cramped and crowded lives that busy people live, and with the security which necessarily bars entry through many doorways.

This need to state things so squarely about relationships reflects the physical as well as human barriers which have sprung up to inhibit human friendships. They are seen in the life of every congregation. Many are managed very well, but when things go wrong there is deep hurt which is not always properly explored.

What opens up friendships?

The Quakers are also known as the 'Society of Friends' – an appropriate alternative title and one which, it is hoped, might come to characterize more and more congregations. Here are a number of characteristics which will encourage congregations to open themselves out in friendship:

- Where the local church has as one of its aims to become a society of friends willing to live with the tension of intimacy and friendship rather than the reserve of congregational anonymity.
- Where permission is given to express affection and discover friendships.
- Where provision is made for close friendships to be made without the need for intimacy to be acted out.
- Where a community can join women's and men's ways of being friends in a way that can meet the needs of both.
- Where an existing intimacy can still allow others to come into the community of friends.

What makes intimacy dangerous?

- When the life of a congregation is defined heavily by the role expectations of its members, office-holders and clergy.
- When the minister is male and the congregation predominantly female.
- When there is a strongly held belief that a lay person has no power to define a relationship.
- When there is no wish for congregation members to move from being helpers to having valued roles of their own.

Celia Hahn[4] says 'Intimacy probably isn't any easier than isolation, but most people find it a good deal more satisfying. Churches which take seriously those who want shoulder-to-shoulder shared enterprise and those who want the mutual exchange of private worlds are churches where members are supported by friendship and who can return to both spheres with renewed energy and courage.'

At its best a congregation can create a hospitable and warming climate which extends the special quality of friendship to all who come within its doors. Both clergy and laity can benefit from an appropriate intimate companionship. Clergy who minister within a community of friends will suffer less stress and isolation. Paradoxically, their vulnerability is reduced while at the same time they are enabled to be more vulnerable.

When the local church becomes a society of friends who live in the tension between intimacy and freedom, it gains women's and men's ways of developing friendships in ways that can meet the needs of both.

Attraction in working relationships

For members of congregations, as well as the rest of the human race, it is not easy to acknowledge feelings of attraction towards people we are 'not supposed' to be attracted to. A number of immediate questions and areas of exploration present themselves. These do not always come at a time when we are able to be rational and explore what is going on inside us.

- There is the need to know what is going on within ourselves before we can begin to make choices or decisions at all.
- There is a need to be honest about my/our own experience and to attempt to behave responsibly.
- There is a need to resist the 'temptation' to act out feelings inappropriately.
- There is a need to be faithful to commitments and contracted relationships, and to a calling.
- There is an overwhelming need to be reminded that sexual relationships belong within marriage or to stable long-term partnerships. 'Making love' is also about living with a partner and sharing duties, trivia, hardships and boredom which are a part of everyday life together.
- Calling is about authenticity and not transparency in role. We may think that we are only deceiving ourselves. Others may be more perceptive.

Attraction and personal growth

Falling in love is quite definitely an occasion of radical spiritual growth. All our feelings are thrown in the air. Our past securities are uprooted. As we come close to another person in intimacy we become changed people ourselves.

Attraction in working relationships, within the congregation as well as elsewhere, raises important ethical issues. The first ones are positive. There is an importance in upholding the goodness of our nature as sexual beings. The American writer Alice Walker in *The Color Purple* says 'God love all them feelings. That's some of the best stuff God did.' We find ourselves caught between an event that seems to *happen* to us and our need to be responsible. The desire to celebrate an intimate relationship is part of our human nature. We have to choose whether public or private celebration is more appropriate to the relationship. The other person needs space. We may show our feelings in no more than supporting the other person in their work or in helping to organize a joint event with them.

Gender and control

We do live in churches where control is a major way of dealing with 'problems'. Churches have a one-sided preoccupation with rules. They instil in many of us a fear of loss of control. Some people will say that there is a men–women difference in dealing with attraction. A male-centred response will have elements of projection. Someone, often the woman, will be blamed for what is taking place. A female-centred response will be more diffuse but will attempt to be holistic. Everything will be seen to be linked to everything else and a wider range of feelings and needs will be brought into consideration.

Falling in love and longing for God

Falling in love is one of the ways heaven tries to break into our hearts. The energy and joy which we experience in meeting another points us towards our meeting with God.

Many of those who come into the ministry of the church have a deep longing to bring a unity into their life experiences. They want to bring together head and heart, body and spirit. In the

Myers–Briggs personality indicators, more than average for the population, ministers have intuitive feelings and temperaments. Many of us have a yearning for an integrating unity for our experiences and in our spirituality. We live with a tension or even a paradox. 'Thou hast put eternity into our hearts' – but not always answers into those longings.

Our cultures are inhibited because there is a loss of vision about how a developed spirituality can contribute to the sense of an emptiness being filled. Love between men and women or between people of the same gender has been substituted. All too often falling in love opens up yearnings which cannot be met by the person who occasions them. A new person capturing our attention looks like a blank cheque for our emotions. Almost always our yearnings are like a promise which cannot be fulfilled by any other person. Here is an invitation to an illusion, it is something like 'falling in love with love'. Life in all its beauty is hinted at in romantic love; but so is loss and despair. What meets us as physical desire, if translated and contained, can become a crucible for our spiritual development and formation within the congregation.

Attraction and misconduct

Sexual misconduct by clergy takes a devastating toll on victims, congregations, offenders and their families, and on entire denominations. Often, by the time a physical sexual interaction has taken place in the clergy–congregation member relationship, the sexual exploitation/violation is but an added trauma to the emotional and spiritual damage already done. The congregation member's sense of abandonment by God and violation by God's emissaries leaves her or him feeling wholly alone and abandoned.

Whenever congregation members encounter clergy, as an officiant in a ritual, or in a visiting or social situation, the minister has a certain 'power' due to transference over another person just by their very presence. Accordingly, it is always the minister's responsibility to be professional in setting and keeping boundaries. We are increasingly aware of the dangers of clergy touching or hugging other adults or of their being alone with children. The natural pastoral gestures of the caring minister have now moved into a zone much more open to misinterpretation. It is the minister's obligation to be conscious of the power s/he has in any relationship with a lay person. It is the professional duty of the minister to stop all sexual behaviour and seductive interaction, whether it is wanted or not.

The abuse of children

One of the most emotive of difficulties arises when advantage is taken of children by those who hold a responsibility for them. In every denomination, as in every voluntary organization, national legislation now makes statutory requirements of those who work with children. Declarations have to be made at the time of appointment and thorough checks made. Each congregation is now advised to appoint two people who hold a watching brief on this subject. They should be as independent as possible and not be the minister, churchwardens or senior stewards.

There are particular features relating to child abuse which churches need to know about. A congregation is always vulnerable to the person who turns up offering to help. When desperate for an organist, it is all too easy to welcome the newcomer without taking care to check where they have come from and the reasons for their leaving their last church.

Difficulties for Christians also arise when a person admits former offences but goes on to say that now they have become a Christian, all that is in the past. We would want to believe them. Forgiveness is an essential part of the life of a Christian community. All the advice from those in the caring professions is towards caution. A completely changed life is a possibility but the primary concern must be for the young people in the life of a church.

A great personal difficulty in faith comes from the person who has acted inappropriately. It seems to be in the area of knowing what is wrong. Very many advisers and therapists will say that offenders did not feel a great sense of guilt in what they were doing because their lives continued to prosper. A response such as 'I felt this could not be wrong if God continued to bless me in other parts of my life and ministry' is made quite frequently. A continual watchfulness and the open avenues to authority and counselling now have to be available. Denominations should have specially appointed Child Protection and Child Abuse Officers in districts and dioceses who should be consulted at the earliest stage if accusations are being made.

When clerical trust is betrayed

As soon as a misdemeanour becomes public, or even when there are suppressed rumours, anger is the first emotion to emerge. When the victims are children there may not be as much anger focused on them as on their parents or those responsible for their care. It is surprising how much those who think that a priest or the leader of a young people's activity 'could not do such a thing' become angry with a victim or the family.

In the case of adults, denial, anger and blame directed towards the victim are common. Beliefs focus around 'the victim asked for it' or that the exploitation was more likely an affair between consenting adults.

Whenever people sense that something terrible has happened, but are told little, displaced anger comes into its own. It really is very hard for people to become angry with their minister in these situations. Instead they transfer their anger to either the victim, or the bishop or authority figure in a denomination.

The source of anger at the authority figure is similar to the anger in incest families aimed at the parent who failed to protect. In addition a lot of damage can result if he or she is perceived to be indifferent to the congregation's pain. By far the most damaging leadership response is to protect the perpetrator beyond the point which is appropriate. The importance of being willing to tell a congregation what has happened cannot be emphasized enough. Alongside this, guarding the victim's privacy is vital.

Anger may continue well into the term of the next minister. It often takes the form of irrational arguments, especially where boundaries between clergy and laity are concerned. People do not know where they are any more. A whole new set of ground rules have to be explored and established.

The congregation is a unique system in any society. Though some of its dynamics and language evoke a family system, the congregation is perhaps better understood as a community of faith. When the person who most embodies the divine for the congregation breaks that trust, faith is shaken. People must know the truth of the events so that they can see where to place their anger. Furthermore, when a few know but most do not, as the years go by a wedge is driven between people in a congregation which can deepen into a chasm. Anger which remains, and

is undischarged, drains people. It results in hope-less congregations and drained clergy.

Boundary violations and outrage

Often, by the time a physical interaction has taken place in a
clergy–lay relationship emotional and spiritual damage has
already been done. The deep outrage within a violated person is
that they feel abandoned by God. A person in authority has
already betrayed trust and abused power. That same person will
have been a figure who has most probably been influential in
accompanying that lay person on their spiritual journey. They
have put trust in their spiritual guide both through the spirituality which they have displayed and through the representative
position they hold in the community of the congregation. That
a clergyman or woman has broken a contract of mutual trust can
easily be seen as an equal betrayal by God when a situation which
had once been the bearer of joy, hope and Christian love suddenly becomes a gaping void.

Causes of clergy misconduct

For very many more clergy than care to admit it, the sense of
loneliness and vulnerability can contribute to the opportunity
for a forbidden activity. The clerical life is an odd one as well as
a fulfilling one. Increasingly, clergy find themselves treated as a
race apart where ordinary friendships cannot be allowed. Some
clergy forbid themselves this basic human need. Then, when
genuine acts of kindness are shown, repressed feelings come to
the surface and uncharacteristic behaviour results. What is said
of clergy can be equally true for any other member of a congregation.

For many clergy a ministry, often shared fully with a partner,
suddenly has a secret part to it. The feeling of leading a double
life can result. Such situations can only be shared with the other
person in the new relationship. Even those in a congregation who
might suspect that something has gone astray find themselves on
unfamiliar territory and do not know the right course of action
to take. A conspiracy of silence at an early stage may well allow
a caring friendship to develop into something dangerous. Equally, gossip which is ill-informed and jealous can cause great harm

if unfounded. The innocent find it hard to recover from completely false allegations. There are some who have been scarred for life and whose long-term relationships have been destabilized.

What to do when suspicion is aroused

No doubt the most difficult area surrounding this subject is what to do when there is an idea that a relationship between others seems to have slipped beyond reasonable boundaries. We all need to know that once a public accusation has been made it never goes away. Even when people are completely cleared of any accusation the slate is never wiped clean. Our memories cannot go back to where they were before. Permanent damage has been done and lives damaged.

A suspicion of any kind needs to be contained in as small a ring of confidentiality as is possible. Someone in a position of responsibility has to be consulted; unfortunately, it also has to be a matter of judgement whether that person can maintain confidentiality. The best, but subjective, test of this can only come through experience. A group of people who have worshipped and shared previous crises together learn who can and who cannot be trusted with a confidence. When those who are under suspicion should be 'sounded out' is also a matter of judgement. The balance is that between causing deep hurt and offence if it is all unfounded and that of helping those becoming involved to pull back before other boundaries are crossed.

A faithful, not a fearful response

The issues surrounding relationships between clergy and congregations are infinitely complex. Only when people have faith in their ability to place trust in all of our clergy can they have the confidence that will help to ease the pain and fear plaguing our world. Our societies need clergy to be effective pastors, priests, and spiritual counsellors. Church leaders, congregations and clergy have always to be working at appropriate role boundaries within faith community relationships. The ways forward towards resolution of clergy sexual boundary violations are through openness, trust and love, not through sanctions, anger, guilt and authority figures choosing to keep it all to themselves.

Congregations are places for real friendship

Because of the extreme caution which has to be exercised in public relationships and in any contact with children, it might seem that all inhibitions are locked in place and congregations cannot be real places to develop relationships in community. The inclusive vitality of many Christian groups gives the lie to this. Congregations are places where people can find real and lasting friendship. These human contacts reflect the relationship which we can have with God through Jesus Christ.

Such maturing relationships should go some way to model personal and community relationships in our wider societies. Congregations, with their web of intricate and intimate human relationships, do work! To believe this we just have to look at who is in them and at why those people stay.

They do work and have in them the single, the lonely, the bereaved, parents whose children live miles away, and vice versa. The bereaved and damaged join because, when it works, the members of a congregation have learned to share intimacy, to be supportive in appropriate ways, to pray together and for one another. Above all, looking from the other end, congregations are held together by people who have caught something of a vision of wholeness, a vision which in its everyday richness speaks of the hope of the Kingdom of Heaven, a place where the quality of relationships will certainly be defined by friendship with God and not by the powerful roles played out by us all on the way.

Notes

1   Celia Allison Hahn, *The Intimate Church* (Action Information, May/June 1992).
2   Wendy Wright, 'Reflections on spiritual friendship between men and women', *Weavings*, 11, no. 4, p. 18.
3   Sally McFague, *Metaphorical Theology* (Philadelphia: Fortune Press, 1982), p. 180.
4   Hahn, *op. cit.*

7

Understanding the
Nuts and Bolts

I once had a work consultant who told me that I would have been happier playing with Meccano than with Lego. He was quite right. I have a great interest in not just constructing things so that they stand there, I like to make things which work. In adult life this is what has brought me to look more closely at congregations. I do not see them as static constructions but as working organizations there to do a task. What is equally interesting about congregations is that not only do they work in different ways, but they also understand who they are differently according to how they regard their parent church.

This chapter is one of the most exciting for me because it allows me to take a look at different structures and theological understandings of church and it allows me to look sideways at what others have said about how organizations understand themselves. I can also look at the voluntary nature of commitment which is at the heart of congregational life and at some of the conflicts which arise when congregations move from wanting to be static to wanting to be working organizations.

Common foundations

The life of members of congregations is underpinned in two different ways. The first, although not articulated by many, is the theology which gives rise to a certain view of what a church is or what it would be like. I want to set out some of those understandings in the early part of this chapter. The second is to do with the standard at which tasks and duties need to be performed and the ways attitudes which need to prevail actually do prevail for a congregation to 'work' – with or without a minister.

The ministry of all the baptized

It is now a commonly understood feature of congregational life in denominations and in ecumenical conversations that, from a response to our baptismal promises, we all share in the ministry of the local church and in God's ministry in the world. People are called to different roles and tasks as a part of that ministry. Much greater responsibility for the life of a local congregation is to be taken by lay people. The place of those who are ordained is now different both within a congregation and in the community. Clergy have a different place in church and in society. Some feel that it is a diminished role or a marginalized place. I have no doubt that doors still open to men and women because they are ordained and that our ministers have a valued place in society which is much greater than the size of our churches might command. There are also places in the secular world where clergy need to be. These are in specialist ministerial roles of a variety of kinds.

There has been an understandable caution about using words like professional and voluntary to describe the way we work within the church. One of the basic strengths of our congregations is their spirit of committed amateurism. This cultural characteristic is a part of the glory of congregational life. The way in which willing volunteers can have a valued and responsible place in the life of the local church is part of its essence. Many have gone on to local and national prominence through what they have learned about leadership and public speaking in their local church.

In coming to understand about internal church ministry there is a concern that in many places voluntary contributions of time are abused. In other situations people hold on to their responsibilities for far too long. Others will not take on church jobs, or take them on again, because they fear that they may be taking on a commitment for life! A look at how we organize our congregations is, to some extent, what this book is about. What is being explored, and sometimes analysed, is the practice of what it is we offer ourselves to do.

Ministry is not a word to be limited to congregational life or to work within the church. Christian ministry is something we do and give freely as a way of working out our faith. Most Christians will exercise their Christian ministry, or their ministries, in making the most of their God-given gifts in the world – in their everyday jobs, their family life and in their leisure. A few will feel called, or will be called by their churches, to an internal, recognized ministry. Very many more people will give of their free time to help run and maintain a local church with its many activities and expect no reward at all.

Such a willing giving of time can be misunderstood and abused. There is a sobering story of the wife with a husband who spent too much time doing odd jobs down at the church. She told a friend that she needed her vacuum cleaner mended at home but her husband never had the time. The friend told her to take it down to the church and it would be mended the next day!

We often get our priorities wrong and lose the sense of balance about how much time to put into congregational activities. Many people have always given uncritically of their time to their local church and this offering will always be valued and respected. Increasingly a confusion is emerging as new ways of developing and energizing lay ministries have emerged and as clergy have tried to be more participative in how they organize their congregations. We have looked at this as we explored collaborative ministry. It is now time to approach this same question from the perspective of an understanding about how churches work.

Understanding our models of church

We need to look at how congregations become 'visionary' and at why denominations have different congregational characteristics. This is our next important task. It is that background understanding of the church which we must explore, if only briefly, before we can understand how the 'culture' or ambience of a denomination is formed and how it might be better served. One of the most influential writers on this subject is Avery Dulles SJ. His work *Models of the Church*, first published in 1975, with an expanded edition in 1988, has given us a platform upon which to construct ideas about how denominations understand themselves and how they function.[1] The use of 'model' in his title comes from thinking about what is now known as 'systems thinking'. It has helped us develop the idea that ways of behaving within a denomination and its structures can be pulled together and described in coherent ways.

This use of such models for us arises from a study of what churches are and how they work – called 'ecclesiology'. Traditionally, ecclesiology has dealt in images rather than in models. Dulles says that the Church Fathers from Origen to the Venerable Bede saw the church in Eve, in Mary, in Abraham and Sarah, in Tamar, Rahab, Mary Magdalene, in the woman with a haemorrhage, the Ark of Noah, the Temple, the Vine and many more. The problem with such images as these is how to distinguish between their proper and their metaphorical use.

By introducing this discussion we have moved on into the sphere of religious imagery. This is both practical and to do with our mental self-understandings. Where Dulles is particularly helpful is that he insists that to be really effective, images have to be rooted in the corporate experience of faithful people. Part of the contemporary crisis of faith is a difficulty with the images which Western believers use to contain or manifest their faith. The theologian and philosopher Paul Tillich said that images are not created or destroyed by deliberate human effort. They are born and they die. They acquire and lose power by a process beyond our comprehension. The models which Dulles sets out are his understanding of how church is expressed in the theology, ministries and structures of some of our major denominations. He himself writes from a perspective of the Roman Catholic Church.

The church as institution

Churches, or more properly, the church, can be understood as a divine organization, established by God as the means by which we come to know anything of him. In this understanding Dulles says its adherents will describe the church as teaching, sanctifying and governing. In its teaching role the church safeguards and preserves the sacred doctrines which God has revealed to us in Christ. These teachings are once-and-for-all. What the church does in passing them on is to add an authority and an interpretation to these teachings which it sees as unalterable. In sanctifying the people of God the church is understood as the way in which grace is mediated. Salvation is offered to the believer through the divine teachings and through the priest-offered sacraments of forgiveness, reconciliation and Holy Communion. It is but a short step to say that there is no path to salvation but through the church. Such an understanding is just what the Reformers rebelled against. They built upon a new sixteenth-century belief that no church or priest can come between a man and his maker, thus creating a new image or model of a 'people's church'. When the church governs, Dulles says, rather than in the teaching and sanctifying functions, the hierarchy of the church have a ministerial function, transmitting the doctrine and grace of Christ himself; ruling is something they do in their own name. They govern the flock, and as Christ's vice-regents, impose new laws and restrictions.

A characteristic of this institutional model of the church is the hierarchical concept of authority. Dulles says: 'The church is not conceived as a democratic or representative society, but as one in which the fullness of power is concentrated in the hands of a ruling class that perpetuates itself by co-option.'

The church as sacrament

Dulles also talks of the church as a sacrament. To those in the church they are a means of grace – outward, visible signs of an inward, invisible contact or communion with God. Through baptism and Holy Communion the church offers forgiveness and a new beginning through closeness to God. We cannot administer these sacraments ourselves. They arise from the God-given work of the Christian community. Dulles says that in this role the church is itself a sacrament. One of the Reformation arguments, now interestingly taking place in radical parts of the Roman Catholic Church, was whether there could be salvation *only* through the sacraments mediated by the church. It is now much more widely understood and accepted that God's gifts are not confined to people who employ biblical or Christian symbolism.

The strength of the concept of church as sacrament is in its social outworkings. Believers do need to meet together in fellowship and for support. Sacraments bring the things of the world, 'the stuff of life' – bread and wine, the water of baptism – into this human contact with God. They press us to know that God is present in all creation, that the needs of the world press in upon the Christian community as it meets together, preventing any possibility of exclusiveness. Symbolic expressions of grace are never adequate to the life of grace itself. Dietrich

Bonhoeffer wrote of 'costly grace', the profession of which has to be meant by the believer and searched for like buried treasure in a life of engagement with the world. In a wonderful phrase, Emil Brunner says of the sacraments that they are independent of the interpretation of the preacher or of whatever a congregation can do with the Word of God. 'One may so interpret the words of scripture that they speak the opposite of their intent; but the Sacraments, thank God, speak a language independent of the minister.'

The church as herald

The church as herald differs from the church as sacrament in that it gives prominence to the Word of God and its proclamation. A herald is one who receives an official message with the commission to pass it on. In a decade of evangelism this understanding of church, which has a primary task of confronting the world with the person of Christ and of passing on the received Christian faith, has come into a new significance. Ideas of the church as an institution have much less prominence to Christians with the herald model. Similarly the importance of a priesthood and hierarchy of specially commissioned and authorized people gets much less prominence. The idea of a local community of believers meeting together has much more importance than a relationship with dioceses or with the worldwide church.

Indeed, believers do not see themselves primarily as belonging to a church with sacraments and order and all the rest. They belong to Christ, and their responsibility as believers and disciples in the world is to him. Faith rather than community or communion is what is most important. Believers find their unity in faith, a unity around the message of the Gospel and in the Word of God.

In recent times the personal, individualistic relation to God has been set alongside the need for believers to relate together in a much stronger, congregational form of fellowship. This often cuts across denominations if the allegiance to Christ takes on a charismatic form of worship. Communal, connexional, associational belief needs organization, not least for security against less 'pure' forms of the faith and, more hopefully, for Christian service in the world.

The church as servant

A church which is endowed with proclamation cannot ignore its responsibilities of *diakonia,* of service in the world. Throughout the whole tradition of Christian belief there has always been an important strand demanding service to those in need.

In the models so far described the primary position is given to the world as the object of Christian mission or service or teaching. With the concept of church as servant the roles are reversed. Just as Christ came to serve, heal, reconcile and bind up wounds, so the church and Christian people in their lives are called to live after his example. Indeed, many would say that the church can have no credibility unless it is first seen to be ordering its life and its structures in this way.

More than that, individual service is not reckoned to be enough. The church, or the churches as institutions will set out their stalls to promote the pursuit of peace, the alleviation of poverty, the promotion of justice, the elimination of racism and the reconciliation of nations. With some awkwardness of late such a stance has been articulated for us all by the World Council of Churches. The defensiveness with which some of its statements and publications are greeted can sometimes be understood as a reflection of the preferred inwardness of church life.

Bishop John Robinson, writing in *The New Reformation,* in a Merlin-like chapter called 'Starting from the other end', shares the view foreshadowed by Teilhard de Chardin and Dietrich Bonhoeffer that the churches must strip away their inhibiting, self-perpetuating structures and become the church of the Servant King working with intimate involvement in the world. 'The house of God is not the church but the world. The church is the servant, and the first characteristic of a servant is that he lives in someone else's house and not his own.'[2] We will always be the church in the world. The practice of our ministries, inside or outside our congregations, is about how well we do what we do.

Dulles has put into what are now classical church words descriptions of the ecclesiology or Meccano-like workings of our churches. Many of the 'popular' management gurus of our present day write about similar organizational characteristics, some of them using near-religious language.

The learning organization

The only way to begin to understand congregations is to try and analyse how they operate as an organization. One thing will come from such an examination. It is that a congregation, or any other organization, is continually learning from reflecting on the way in which it operates. One of the most influential pieces of thinking from a modern 'prophet' about how organizations learn has come from Peter Senge while Director of the Systems Thinking and Organizational Learning Programme at the Sloane School of Management at Massachusetts Institute of Technology. His book *The Fifth Discipline*[3] has a provocative and stimulating way of helping organizations to understand how they learn. He writes about the characteristics of 'the learning organization'. They have definite parallels with life in our congregations.

The disciplines are these:

- *Personal mastery.* This is the discipline of continually clarifying and deepening our personal vision. It is a dynamic activity, never satisfied with the present but always wanting to clarify what is happening now in order to move on to a next objective, dream or vision.
- *Mental models.* These are deeply ingrained assumptions, generalizations or even pictures and images which influence how we understand the world. They help to give a 'corporate image' to a company or an identity to a group in society. The models of church set out by Avery Dulles earlier in this chapter come into this category.
- *Building shared vision.* When there is a shared vision, owned by the majority of the members of an organization (as opposed to the all-too-familiar 'mission statement') people achieve high standards and go on learning, not because they are told to, but because they want to. Churches often develop around the charisma of a popular leader. They continue to grow and become stabilized when that vision and charisma is shared among the wider group.
- *Team learning.* When a group of people are working well, and in a co-ordinated way, their collective intelligence often exceeds that of any one individual. When people are willing to help one another out, learn from mistakes, share in the

enthusiasm for an idea, then the whole group or team is learning in a creative way.

* *Systems thinking.* Senge calls his book *The Fifth Discipline* because he says that he is sure it is in an integration of thinking and disciplines that the whole comes together in its most creative and learning way. Systems thinking needs the other disciplines in order to come alive. Building a shared vision fosters a commitment to the long term. Mental models focus on the need to unearth shortcomings in the way the world is seen at the moment. Team learning develops the skills of people who look for the larger picture that lies beyond individual perspectives. Personal mastery fosters the personal motivation to continually learn how our actions affect the world around us. These elements are integrated by the learning process implicit in systems thinking.

In this completely secular book, with references to spirituality, Senge ends up by talking about *metanoia* – a shift of mind. He says that his observations of people in learning organizations is that of people talking about a 'golden age' in their lives, when a particular group of people came together and were able to create an atmosphere which was something special. In biblical terms *metanoia* has come to be understood as repentance. Senge comments that to grasp the deeper elements of learning in organizations is to understand that a shift of mind has taken place. it cannot be constructed. No group can say 'We are a learning organization'. The change has a magical quality which is experienced when other key factors are all in play. Those in a congregation which has a 'buzz' about it have experiences just like this.

Standards

A different but important way to look at how we work together in congregations is to look at the levels by which we perform our tasks, within whichever view of church we are working. I want to suggest two ways in which levels of effectiveness might be raised by a congregation. A group of clergy in the Nottingham area have looked at the number of people and processes involved in the preparation of a child for baptism.[4] They analysed the meetings which might begin either with the minister or the parish secretary and have traced all the contacts, through preparation classes with congregation members, to the service and follow-up visits. This group took the British Standard about quality assurance in relation to customers and applied it to what should be expected, or provided, for parents as they pass through this chain of church contacts. The analysis of who meets who and in what capacity is fascinating, as is the understanding of what can be expected through each contact. They have taken their work on much farther since then through Investors in People and with other publications.

Even more engaging is a suggestion made by David Jesset in *Ministry*[5] that a local church might consider a 'Parishioner's Charter'. He suggests that a congregation could set itself standards and that these might be measured against actual performance. Such suggestions may seem basic but it is stunning to realize how few local congregations and church buildings might measure up to them. He suggests by way of examples:

- *Worship*: A church council and minister might guarantee to parishioners that all services will be clearly advertised and will start on time.
- *Administration*: A parish might decide it should have a standard that all letters which arrive with the vicar or church council will get a reply within a week, that all committee minutes will be circulated within a week after the meeting and that all agendas are sent out within ten days of the next meeting.
- *Pastoral care*: Here it might be guaranteed that everyone who is notified as ill to the minister or parish office will be visited by someone from the church within a week.

The list can be extended but those characteristics of parish and congregational life are perhaps sufficient to give a local church the idea of what might be on its own 'Parishioner's Charter'.

Building blocks to change

Congregational inertia is the principal stumbling-block to change of any kind. In the case of collaborative ministry the main obstacle is a collusion between laity and clergy to keep things as

they are, with the minister carrying out too many of the key organizational roles. Clergy will go along with this because it keeps
them at the 'centre' and gives the feeling that they are getting
things done. Laity will go along with this because they feel that
they are getting a clear lead, that the clergy are in the right place
and, of course, because they are excused from the trouble of
thinking and from the risk of having to take on actual responsibility. The consequence of such collusion is that roles become
stereotyped, everything hangs upon the energy and the vision of
the minister, and laity who want to take responsibility or do
things in a different way vote with their feet. The truth of the
matter is that such situations are no longer viable. Circumstances have forced change upon every congregation. In many
places across the world lively congregational life is sustained
without the regular presence of an ordained person at all.

Life and work in the non-clergy-centred congregation

The biggest difference world-wide in the shape of a local congregation is the absence of a resident, paid minister. Whether the
circumstances are financial or caused by the drop in vocations to
the ordained ministry, or those of a church which is growing
more rapidly than the supply of ministers, there will not be an
ordained person on the ground. Such a situation causes anxiety
for many reasons. The origin of many of these is theological. The
concept of oversight in an episcopally ordered church implies
that bishops, priests and deacons will be a part of the structure
in the national and the local church. They will exercise oversight
of a pastoral nature. Control will often also be exercised in manifestations of varying rigidity. A church which cannot maintain
this system has severe problems. These approaches or changes
may be being sent from God and ought to be seen as opportunities: not the opportunities which would want to overthrow the
old order but the opportunities which ask us to look again at how
we use people called out and set apart in particular ways.
Churches which have, as a main part of their history, a congregational emphasis are not exempt from putting their minister in
a similar central place with all the temptations to collusion and
autocracy which go with it.

The phrase 'non-staff dependent' is an appropriate one. It
appeared in an article by William Jones in the Alban Institute

journal, *Congregations*.[6] Jones described the move from a church where he was the centre of all activities – indeed many did not go on properly if he were not there – to a congregation where responsibility was shared and where the minister was only expected to be present on certain understood occasions. He wrote about his previous congregation which was a full and busy one where he had experienced 'burn-out' twice. Being at the centre of every parish activity, and the initiator of most, simply exhausted him. The move to a new congregation, where in many ways at first he felt that he was not needed, led him to reflect:

- Who needs to make up the agendas and call the meeting?
- Why did he feel the need to be present at every meeting?
- How did he feel when he found that groups met without him?
- Who should be responsible for following up decisions made at meetings?
- How protective and controlling did he need to be for his own sense of well-being?

Such questioning and discoveries, caused by a move into a different ecclesiastical culture, led to an even more interesting question: 'Who thinks for the congregation?' Answers to this will help us all to move from the deeply ingrained culture of dependence in many congregations to situations, and a culture, where Christians, in learning organization terms, think, plan and execute work together in ways which are based on another set of assumptions.

The virtual absence of clergy in many situations will create the situations where this kind of thinking can flourish. The transition from current structures and situations to this new world is difficult and will cause tremendous stress. For churches where there are resident clergy there are equally important questions here about role and the rightness of taking on a whole range of tasks which need not necessarily be done by an ordained person. Churches do not grow most rapidly when the minister is the omni-competent centre of the hub. At the centre, yes, but radiating from the minister are the resources and affirmations which make change and adaptation to a new situation possible. Ultimately, it is our attitudes to change and our willingness to put ourselves in the place of, or alongside, others which will determine the spirituality within ourselves and in the characteristics of the communities to which we belong. Hence the need to approach transition and change in the spirit of service rather than that of conflict or of defensiveness.

Conflict and the practice of ministry

One of the greatest tests of professionalism and of the use of training and skills is seen in how a congregation deals with conflict. How can a congregation get to where it wants to be and how can a majority of its members be held together? How can this journey be made in a way that others, not in the life of the church at all, can see another way of living together through stretching and demanding times? The great achievement for any group is to be able to move from one place or situation to another and be able to stay together. The example of Moses leading his people through the wilderness has to be the very best example for us here. Different views have to be reconciled and people will want to change, if at all, at different paces. More than almost everything else, change will bring anxiety and a level of insecurity. While a congregation, and its minister, are adapting to change or a new set of circumstances, they are in transition. This stage of development needs to be recognized and worked with in ways which will enable everyone to contribute.

No minister or group will get everything right. Indeed with hindsight many will say either that they are pleased they did not know all they had to go through, or that the experience was like tiptoeing through a minefield. I once went to a concert where the choir president said the performance had only been so very good because there had been so many disasters on the way!

Transition and change have to be faced by all of us. On one level change is brought about by the inability of internal life to be able to carry on as it had done before. At another level change is about putting things right or making organizational adjustments in a place or a congregation where things are not being done as effectively as they might and where conflict rather than co-operation is the overriding factor.

Common sources of conflict

People disagree about values and beliefs

Congregations will disagree about what the church is and what it ought to be about. Such disagreement will mean that the vision of the church is unclear. Consequently the congregation will not have worked out its goals or objectives. If statements have been made in everyone's name without their real consent there will be frustration that little action results from them.

The way through this is to spend much more time than the enthusiasts would like in consulting and listening to all those involved. Only when there is a high feeling of opinion being heard, if not necessarily acted on, will the reluctant come along and ownership be felt by almost everyone.

The structures are unclear

In churches and congregations without clear structures no one is sure what to do and no one is sure what anyone else is supposed to do. There are no understood agreements or guidelines about the roles and responsibilities of clergy, staff, lay people or church committees. This lack of clarity is a constant source of conflict. Because no one is sure what to do, either nothing gets done because no one will take responsibility, or nothing seems to be achieved because one group or person will continually challenge the activity of the others. I was once asked to spend time with a congregation where the meetings were adequate but nothing happened afterwards. While sitting-in on the meetings I soon discovered that clear decisions could not be made in many cases because there was insufficient information available on which to make a decision. On other occasions, at the end of what seemed like a productive discussion, the question 'So who will take responsibility for this?' was never asked. At best it was assumed that the vicar would pick up this responsibility. When nothing had happened by the next meeting, anger and frustration became frequent visitors.

Structures can also be obscured or invalidated in congregations where one group will continually disregard the agreed way of doing things. People who are unwilling to work within an agreed structure can be influential and visionary; they can also enjoy the frustration and confusion caused by their actions.

One way forward is for lines of accountability to be clear and for those who have executive authority to act responsibly and use the powers given to them to keep people and groups within agreed structures and courses of action. This is not a recommendation for stultifying bureaucracy but a recognition that carefully worked out and agreed structures can enable change as well as prevent it. As churches grow they will need agreed structures more and more. Even small and family-sized congregations need to have structures which are in place, understood and respected.

The structures no longer fit the size of the congregation

Increases in numbers can be a great source of joy: it is what most congregations say that they want. However, a change in size can be a source of trouble and conflict. A congregation which is growing, or is shrinking, often finds itself operating in a way that is inappropriate for its present size. If a congregation is smaller than it used to be, it often tries to operate as it did in the past. It will have too many committees and activities which put a tremendous strain on the smaller remaining number of willing people. It is often helpful for an outsider, or a senior member of the denomination, to come in and act as a consultant to rationalize a situation which those within it are unable to face.

In churches which are growing, a different situation obtains. There is a well-remembered time 'when everybody knew everybody and the minister was able to call'. Now life within the congregation is more likely to take place in small groups and tasks are carried out by members who are not well known to everyone. The minister is surrounded by an overwhelming set of expectations. An appropriate way forward here is for there to be occasional times when all the congregation are able to meet together, to socialize, to meet newcomers and to negotiate the expectations put on leaders. There needs to be a celebration of the growth which has taken place and some measure of consensus that if growth is to continue then people, and that includes the minister, will have to act in different ways – both to survive and also for the whole ministry of the congregation to be effective.

Clergy and parish styles are in conflict

Congregations which are in trouble often try to focus the problem on the style of ministry of the priest. Clergy relate to congregations in very different ways. What is most crucial is for the right kind of minister to come to a congregation at the right time in its life. Clergy who are very active are right for times of growth and change. They will not fit well into a congregation which needs consolidation after a rapid time of change.

Extremely pastoral person-centred clergy will do well at times when congregations need to be nursed or when previous troubles need to be healed. They will be resented if the appropriate style needed for that phase is a person who will grasp nettles, 'see the trouble makers off' and establish new working practices.

Conflict, which is not brought on by a new minister, can arise where a very long-stay priest is being followed. Surprisingly large numbers of such people do not remain long in post. This is either because a congregation is still grieving the loss of the last minister or that person's style of ministry has become so ingrained that only years of patient listening and encouragement will prevent an explosion or turn a congregation from terminal grieving decline.

The new minister rushes into changes

All congregations are both keen to welcome their new minister and anxious about what changes will be made. Many clergy arriving in their new situations do not take enough time to get to know their people before rushing to make changes. Frequently, these changes are not enormous and shocking, they are tiny things, which are brought in without explanation. Most members of a congregation are reluctant to ask a minister why changes are being made. Some changes are unwitting. A minister will be doing what they have always done, or have brought a practice they liked from their previous congregation. It will feel like continuity and familiarity to them but will appear as change and innovation to the new congregation.

Visiting, talking, explaining, questioning will go some way to overcoming this, as will asking people what they like about new practices where difference is voiced. The minister who introduces 'The Peace' to a communion service and who walks around sharing it in a congregation unfamiliar with the practice will be brave and liberating to some or, more likely, will be bruised and blamed by many!

Change can best be brought about by the minister who has developed the necessary level of trust and understanding with a congregation and who has been able to involve others in the decisions and actions which are necessary to bring about change.

Lines of communication are blocked

It is easy to blame problems in a congregation on loss of communication or on bad communication. Often communication problems are more the *result* of conflict than the cause of it.

When conflict arises or escalates, members of one faction or group tend to try to avoid contact or communication with others. There is almost a need for steps to be taken to prevent conflict hardening and attempts made to exaggerate difference and create scapegoats.

Often, in a troubled congregation, the minister and church council think that by withholding information they are helping to defuse a situation. In fact, they are allowing distortions to grow and are creating a vacuum where false rumours can grow up.

One very good way to take the tension out of a situation is to offer 'open forum' meetings, perhaps facilitated by an outsider, where a balance of feelings and opinions can be expressed in a structured and controlled way. If people can meet face-to-face, it is much more difficult to maintain absolute positions and it is possible to begin shared discussions about ways forward. Those who stay away from such consultations become marginalized and either leave or try to find a face-saving way back in. Here a consultant or sensitive minister can be a great asset.

People manage conflict badly

Many churchpeople hold the unspoken view that conflict is bad and should not be acknowledged or allowed to happen. 'Even if conflict is there we will not recognize it.' The best response to such situations is to spread a 'good news about conflict' message:

- Conflict is a part of everyday life and is neither good nor bad.
- Conflict creates the energy which makes change possible.
- Conflict only becomes destructive when it is mismanaged.
- Well-managed conflict is hardly recognized as such, it is experienced as a release of energy
- Conflict which is resolved by negotiation is often experienced as a 'Win–win' situation where both or all sides feel

that they have gained something without giving away anything vital and without an awkward compromise of
principle.

- When conflict is denied, so also is the opportunity to deal
  with it in constructive ways.
- Avoidance of conflict causes 'triangling' where a third person
  is told about a situation and invited to sympathize or collude.
- When conflict is denied, anger is not released and becomes
  embittering and inwardly destructive.

Disaffected members hold back resources

Change causes people to want to hold on to what is seen by them
as security. This becomes particularly apparent when those who
control a group or an area of finance will not let go. It is equally
significant when a person is responsible for a part of the church
building or the hall. They will try to control their physical territory to prevent change making any progress. This province is not
exclusively the territory of the church organist or the hall care-
taker – but they could teach courses on it!

Care, patience, explanations and, occasionally, firmness
which will allow a gracious climb-down are a very good way forward. Unfortunately, the disaffected, like the poor in Our Lord's
phrase, will always be with us. They have a rightful place in any
caring and collaborative community, to be heard; but not a
right to prevent change or to subvert planning exercised with
integrity.

Living with uncertainty and provisionality

The most significant thread running through all accounts of the
causes of conflict is that of change and of uncertainty about the
future. Change is not only taking place within a congregation
and causing anxiety, but it is also taking place in the relationship
of a congregation to its environment – to the community in
which it is placed and to the wider world which is either perceived as indifferent or apathetic. It is seen as a world made up
of Christians who express their faith in very different ways and
of members from other faiths who appear to have a much deeper, even aggressive, commitment to the whole culture which
surrounds belief.

New ways of responding to conflict and change are emerging.

These differences have been described well by Professor Gillian Stamp in an article called 'The enhancement of ministry in uncertainty'.[7] She says that in her experience, when organizations used to work together, even in collaborative ways, to bring about change they would expect that once they had adapted to a new set of circumstances, things would 'settle down' again to the kind of equilibrium which they had previously enjoyed. Her observations are now that organizations are no longer 'making changes' and expecting 'things to calm down again'. It seems that they are saying 'the only thing we can be certain of these days, is uncertainty'. A way of maximizing this realization, rather than seeing it as a deeply pessimistic observation, is to try to work with situations of forced change rather than taking massive stances to resist. For churches this has led to considerable controversy. If too much going with 'the spirit of the age' is experienced then either trendiness, relevance or following moral or intellectual fashion is thrown back. On the other hand, a stubborn defensiveness frequently results in an unwillingness to engage with the ideas and controversies of a changing society and church and a fossilization of organization, belief and structures.

Once again, the concept of a 'learning organization' seems to be required. The congregation which can 'stand back' and ask itself what is happening, what experiences do we have of tension or conflict, how can we listen to one another and to those outside, is the one which is learning and growing through being able to reflect on its place in a changing set of circumstances.

Living with uncertainty and provisionality is, after all, a biblical concept. The 'heroes' of the Old Testament – Moses, Abraham, David and any number of the prophets – moved on in faith to changing circumstances and felt led to do so because of their trust in God. The whole experience of Exile and of self-understanding as 'Remnant' meant that a people and a community of faith had to look at itself again and ask what God is saying in situations of forced change. Jesus continually felt the need to move on. It is a widely held view that the progress of his ministry led Jesus on into deeper situations of conflict until things came to a climax in the last week of his life in Jerusalem. The disciples and followers of Jesus left their own security and followed him in his itinerant ministry. The newly forming church after his resurrection was continually beset by tensions, conflicts and change as expansion faced the Apostles and the newly converted Christians. For many people it seems that the churches are coming to the end of many centuries of settled, cautious conservatism. The atmosphere of many renewed, but still small churches seems to feel more like that of the young churches of the first centuries. Change is being forced by both numerical decline, a re-evaluation of the way belief is expressed and the pressure from growing churches in developing countries who demonstrate that growth and a vibrant faith only begin when the old structures and support systems are swept away.

Movement people

Within this arena of conflict, one of the most sensitive areas in any church is the tension between modernist and traditionalist. This has come to a head over attitudes towards the ordination of women and in relation to charismatic versus liturgical worship. In Sheffield a 'Nine o'clock Service' at first drew attention because of its innovative use of modern media and dance for worship, and later for controversy surrounding the principal minister. Reviewing a book on the controversy in *The Tablet*, Bishop Tom Butler had some interesting words to say about the tensions surrounding change:

> The Church always needs to be renewed by those who have a vision linked to the hopes and aspirations of modern people . . . 'movement people' and 'church tradition people' need each other. The Church always needs to be renewed by those who have a vision linked to the hopes and aspirations of modern people . . . 'movement people' need to value the tradition from which they spring . . . To give 'movement people' a totally free hand because they are more in touch with today's particular time and culture is to court disaster – it is easier to start new ventures than to build on existing structures in such a way as to enable them to be a blessing far into the future . . . a congregation or group that is too dependent on the charisma of a single individual or the vision of a tight controlling group does itself and its tradition no favours: if they are to survive and prosper, ministry and mission need a broad base.[8]

A servant ministry

The idea of servant is deeply embedded in both our Christian culture and our inherited Englishness. It is also a basic theological and ministerial concept. For many Christians, especially around the Easter season, the vision of 'suffering servant' appears on our religious consciousness. The prophet Isaiah described the idea of a servant suffering on behalf of others (chapter 53) and this was picked up and used by Jesus and those who interpreted the significance of his death in the life of the church. The importance of this key gospel concept is that it is God who initiates the one act of redemptive self-offering which is performed by the Servant-Messiah.

Robert K. Greenleaf has devoted a lifetime of management and teaching to this concept of the leader as servant. He begins one of his books with this story.[9] The idea of servant as leader has an engaging manifestation in Hermann Hesse's *Journey to the East*. A band of men set out on a mythical journey. The central figure of the story is Leo who accompanies the party as the servant and who does their menial chores, but who also sustains them with his spirit and his song. He is a person of extraordinary presence, but disappears. Then the group falls into disarray and the journey is abandoned. They cannot make it without the servant Leo. The narrator, one of the party, after some years of wandering finds Leo and is taken into the Order that had sponsored the journey. There he discovers that Leo, whom he had first discovered as servant, was in fact the titular head of the Order, its guiding spirit, a great and noble leader.

Such a story, unusual in concepts of leadership, says that a great leader can also be seen as a servant. Leo was actually the leader all of the time, but he was servant first because that was what he was, *deep down inside*. His role as leader in the Order was something given, or assumed, that could be taken away. His servant nature was the real man, not bestowed, nor assumed, and not to be taken away. The leader of a group, the minister or bishop who has such a characteristic, will be the one who reflects the character and nature of the Master for whom they are truly servants.

Above all others, this idea of redemptive self-sacrifice is what brings many to the life and person of Jesus. To describe him as 'the man for others' is to communicate to believer and nonbeliever at a very deep level. It should come as no surprise then that a way of understanding the life of a congregation should be in these ways of action. Particularly in times of stress and transition it is the willingness to give oneself in listening and service to others which will bring abut redemptive change. This level of spiritual understanding will transcend working methods of collaboration. In a society which has gravitated to self-protection and, even in spiritual journeying, to aims of self-fulfilment the refreshing willingness of self-giving can really make the life of a congregation a model way, if at times misunderstood by the wider community. This is much more than community service and helping others: it is a willingness to give up and give away which will look like weakness and vulnerability to those who do not want to see.

The servant ministry, if it can be called that, is exactly a part of the English culture. Government ministers are called 'civil servants'. In government offices they work in 'ministries'. If ignored by over-familiarity, these public titles are a constant and timely reminder about how people and groups might relate to one another. They stem from roots in the biblical tradition. More significantly the whole idea of service is described in the word *diaconia*. It is not surprising, therefore, that the concept of Christian disciples as *ministers/servants* should have received great emphasis in the early church and its utilization be carried on right up to the present day. As a consequence of Christian baptism it has always been understood that there are no 'lay' members in the church who are without a ministry within it. The central way of working out a ministry is through servanthood, just as Christ saw himself as a servant, giving himself for others. The development of a special order of the Diaconate within the church should not allow this basic idea to be overshadowed. Equally, bishops and priests should never forget that they were first ordained as deacons, and deacons they remain. Christ himself reminded his disciples that when they offer deeds of service to another person in need, they are serving him in the form of that other person. John Robinson has reminded us that 'a servant is always aware of living in someone else's house'.

Service and willingness to serve

In times of crisis and change it is all too easy to retreat into defensive positions and to 'pull up the drawbridge'. No amount of analysis about what is going on in a congregation will make any difference if its members and its clergy are not, at a simple and basic level, prepared to live and minister in a 'Christ-like' way. The essence of that way is to be prepared to approach one other and a world rich in beauty and culture but aching with demands, in the form of a servant ministry. By doing this, those who want to can see the image of what God was doing in Christ in our actions and attitudes. In what other form dare we call ourselves his Body other than as that broken in the service of others? It is the ultimate play on words in the deliberately ambiguous choice of wording in my title *Understanding Congregations*.

Notes

1   Avery Dulles, *Models of the Church* (Gill & Macmillan, 1987).
2   J. A. T. Robinson, *The New Reformation* (SCM, 1965), pp. 32ff.
3   Peter M. Senge, *The Fifth Discipline* (Century Business), pp. 5–15.
4   For full details contact the Southwell Diocesan Office, Dunham House, Westgate, Southwell, Notts NG25 0GL.
5   David Jesset, 'A parishioner's charter', *Ministry*, edition 20 (Summer 1993).
6   William Jones, 'Leadership in a non-staff-dependent congregation', *Congregations* (November-December 1996).
7   Gillian Stamp, 'The enhancement of ministry in uncertainty' (Brunel Institute of Organisation and Social Studies, published paper, 1993).
8   Bishop Tom Butler, 'Shattered dream', book review of *The Rise and Fall of the Nine o'Clock Service*, *The Tablet* (11 January 1997).
9   For a developed exposition of this theme see Robert K. Greenleaf, *Servant Leadership* (Paulist Press, 1991).

8

Understanding
New-shape Congregations

There do seem to be some strong themes which can be identified and named for themselves. They recur so often in the
tremendous range of ideas and models which I have tried to
explore. They appear to be present in the life and memory of any
congregation which has the will to survive and live. Many of
these characteristics are not the province of any one person or
group within a congregation. A minister working with a short
time-span can create few of them, unless they have been given a
special turn-around task. In many ways the visible characteristics we have explored are the tips of icebergs. They show
themselves to us in ways which we can recognize, but they also
represent very much more that is unseen. Some of these are not
special to Christian groups but have characteristics which can be
seen as 'good practice' and as 'barriers to change' in the best and
worst of companies and voluntary organizations.[1]

Analysis and vision

Every good consultant knows that the real part of his or her work
is done in the analysis of a situation. The more one probes and
asks questions of those involved in an organization or a situation,
the more obvious a solution, or a range of options, becomes.
Much of the work is done in the debate and the dialogue. With
such analysis by a consultant there can also be an element of
frustration. Ways forward can be seen, as can the hard or painful
work required to get there. Only when there is an excitement
about a shared vision does the drudgery lift and a new 'buzz' of
infectious enthusiasm take over. In what follows I want to
describe the seven styles of effective survival which my own
analysis of congregations suggests. This is either the 'How to get
there' or the 'What can I use to measure progress?' part of my

own reflection. After that I want to end by sharing my own vision, what makes me excited, about the shape of congregations for the future.

Seven marks of effective survival

1. *Know your own story*
The healthy congregation will neither be afraid of its past nor be fearful for its future.

First and foremost there will be a positive attitude to what has gone before. This includes the bad and the good, the scars and the mountaintop experiences. Previous vicars will be spoken of for what they were: neither worshipped as the hero of a golden past nor condemned as the sole architect of current problems. The history of a congregation will be celebrated and its memories passed on to newcomers and the next generation through the natural arteries of story-telling which exist but cannot ever be created artificially. Photographs and documents from the past will be displayed with pride as a way of assisting and celebrating the memory; but a particular time, people or pieces of furniture will not be venerated!

There will be memories and events in the life of any congregation where there will be an element of embarrassment and stories not fully told. Within all this there will be unanswered questions about possible/probable scandals, some true, most imagined, magnified and perpetuated because the truth was concealed. There are right times to draw a line under such things, to say the past is the past and we shall never know the whole story. Indeed, many of those who could have given the answers will be dead and have left no written record. Others may still hold 'the secrets' and use that knowledge as their own private piece of power.

Exorcizing ghosts is a necessity. Either an occurrence from the past needs to be known about in order for a congregation to move on – or it needs to be acknowledged as no longer *directly* relevant, and consigned to the past. Sometimes this needs to be done publicly, symbolically or liturgically depending on the form of the story.

In one of my own parishes I remember a lady in her eighties being deeply moved when a visiting mission group invited us all to write particular confessions, personal to ourselves, on a piece of paper. We each put our papers into an upturned dustbin lid and they were burned. The symbolism of that particular event moved to tears someone who had seen it all before but who thought she was going to have to carry some pieces of guilt to the grave.

2. Choose to live
A congregation has to want to survive before it can grow and change.

If the will to grow and develop is not there, then decline and ultimate stagnation have to be an inevitable consequence. Unreflective congregations and clergy are frequently heard to comment, with genuine perplexity, about the number of people who come to a church once but who are never seen there again. The Merlin factor about a future dream, hope or reality is directly relevant to Christian living. In our congregational life we live out the truth-giving, creative tension, of a paradox. On the one hand we know that we have a future fulfilled by the presence of the Risen Christ. On the other we struggle to work with God to help reveal or establish the signs of the Kingdom here on earth. Choosing to live means choosing to move towards a future whose shape we shall recognize because we have been given its characteristics in the life, death and resurrection of Christ.

A congregation which wants to show the characteristics of new life is one which adopts that Merlin principle: 'What you choose for your future is more important than what you know about your past or present capabilities.' So, whether we are exploring, as we have done in previous parts of this book, the life cycle of a congregation, or facing conflict, or looking at models of ministry, we know that we shall never be content with what we have, that no view of ministry will completely satisfy us, and that no conflict need, ultimately, be destructive. These things can only be if we have chosen to live as if it were possible for us to have a future which is bigger and richer in our communal life than ever could be predicted from the present analysis of our congregation. If I were asked to select my own records for an imaginary stay on a desert island, I would certainly choose 'We Shall Overcome'. In my view, that ultimate springing up of hope in the most oppressed parts of the human spirit is the very heart of the Christian Gospel.

3. Live with difference
It is the sign of any mature society that it can tolerate difference.

We know from the history of this century, and from the appalling atrocities which have taken place within it, some of the consequences of intolerance. If the Christian congregation is a model of how community life might be, then it has to have, as one of its basic characteristics, the toleration of difference.

One of the key aspects of life and health in a congregation is not that it has different people and groups within it, all should have that; it is how these differing and sometimes competing groups grow and are enriched through dialogue with those who have different opinions and sometimes seemingly different values.

Living with difference will mean that in a congregation of any size there will be those who have very different views of what church is. With increasingly mobile populations some will still have their roots in another denomination. Those in large congregations who hanker for the characteristics of the small, pastoral church will want to know their minister personally and expect to have a particular and regular contact. Others will expect a significant preaching ministry, while again others will want an efficiently run organization. Groups within an open congregation will have found ways of engaging in dialogue with each other about these expectations. There will be those who always feel that they are in the wrong place. Dialogue will show that only a few of us are! The 'mature' congregation will have found ways of compensating and effective ways of providing for the needs of those who feel difference acutely. These will come from other sources or from within their own congregations.

In a similar way, the minister who survives in a growing and many-faceted church will be a person who has learned to balance competing expectations and to live with the tension of differing opinions. The secure pastor, priest, minister, bishop or chairman will act because they feel 'I'm damned if I do – and I'm damned if I don't' and will not be paralysed by their situation. They will have accepted that they can never fully meet their own expectations of ministry, or those of widely differing groups of people within the congregation – let alone the wider community. The ministers who can live with difference are people who will never be complacent and who will never deliberately avoid conflict. They will be people who have an inner ease with themselves because they have a security in their sense of God's call. Such security will enable them to go on and explore with a positive restlessness the questioning and dialogue necessary for difference to develop into creative progress and which will give a vibrant feel to the life of those with whom they minister.

4. Manage change

A congregation which has life and vitality is one which has raised itself from 'drift' and has made constructive attempts to establish a sense of direction.

It will be a congregation, with a minister, which is not afraid to ask for outside help. It will have made frequent use of visiting speakers or missioners and is likely to have a consultant. It will encourage its minister to go away for courses and training – and will not ask if they have had a good 'holiday' when they get back! It will probably have a link with a congregation in a very different social context and a close association with one or more congregations overseas.

Such a willingness to listen to outsiders and to search for a renewed sense of direction will mean that a congregation will have taken the management of change into its systems. Aims and targets will be common coinage. A mission statement is likely to be in place. There will certainly be times when the whole congregation, as well as the church council and its activity groups, take stock and evaluate where they are.

The careful, sensitive, management of change will involve planning. It will mean that a congregation develops a vision of where it wants to go and will have divided the means-to-the-end vision into a series of manageable and achievable tasks.

A congregation which has taken the management of change into itself will also be one which is sensitive to those who want to go at a different pace. Enthusiasts will be impatient and will want to forge ahead. The more cautious will enjoy the security of familiarity and will advise against taking risks. Managing change within a congregation should be an exercise in attempting to take as many people as possible along with a shared vision for the future. To do this will involve consultation and dialogue, and the willingness to give and take, since debate and negotiation involve those who differ being willing both to listen and to be open to the possibility that they do not have all of the truth even on their own subject. When managed well, change will have the 'Win–win' feel to it in that everyone will have gained, will have achieved something of their own position, and will feel enriched by the gifts and graciousness of others. They will have learned more from God about themselves.

Managing change takes time. Dialogue and the attempt to involve as many people as possible in a collaborative exercise is the 'long way round'. It is my belief that these methods of working are the essence of the Christian Gospel. The basic characteristic of any Christian community is one which values each of its members for who they are and which takes each opinion and each need seriously. Such a corporate life only gains momentum when a sense of purpose is shared and when sensitively managed leadership allows change and growth to have both a human and a God-shaped face.

5. Want a renewed spirituality
No effective congregation can have a spirituality which is either wholly locked up in the past or which is totally turned-in on itself.

A congregation which is only keeping alive and defending a tradition – whether it is Anglo-Catholicism, Methodism, Congregationalism or the like – will be feeding a spirituality which met the needs of a past age and culture. It may well have a richness and a great spiritual tradition, but one which can only come alive when it is brought to engage with the issues facing the world and a church of today.

Defensiveness leads to rigidity and an unwillingness to learn from those with whom we think we differ. The history of religions can be read as a history of rivalry and faction where not only denominations but also world faiths appear to conspire to set communities and nations against one another. The other face of those same religious beliefs is not a universalism which reduces faith to a 'believe anything if it suits you' kind of religiosity. Rather, it reveals great treasures in the search for faith and meaning by people of different cultures and with greatly contrasting pasts.

We live in an age, at the momentous turn of the Millennium, when so very many people are willing to explore other than material elements in their lives. The congregation which is secure in the spirituality of its tradition but which is willing to risk its development by bringing prayer and worship into play with the religious experience of others, is one which will convey the atmosphere of a living spiritual search. It will be one where the experience of working life is celebrated and where the spiritual dimensions of work will be explored. It will be a place where the searcher and the explorer will meet the traditionalist and the mystic, and it will be the place where each will feel themselves to be somewhere between the Mount of Transfiguration and the second distance-marker on the Emmaus Road.

6. Be a learning organization
The learning organization or congregation will display the capacity to move and to change.

It will strive continually for a clarifying and a deepening of its personal understanding. Lent and Advent courses will be features in the process of self-understanding, as will be the opportunity for the congregation, or individual parishioners, to go away for times of silence and retreat. The learning will also take the form of a continuous striving to improve on the standards offered in worship and in service. Like the craftsman always looking for improvement, so also the choir, the altar party and servers, the sewing and fabric groups will keep on at the attempts to improve what they offer to their church. This learning and reflecting task within service will be a mark of the church concerned about the standard of what is offered to God.

The learning congregation will never be satisfied with the concepts or 'models' that it has accepted for itself. There will be a constant process of redefining who they are and what they are there for. Questions will keep on being asked about whether or not the agenda of the world is shaping the agenda for the church and whether the churches and their congregations can influence, by their behaviour, the ways in which local and national communities understand themselves.

There will be an energetic desire to build a shared vision. The enthusiasm of the early stages in the life cycle of a congregation will continue to break out as new groups are formed and as new members join. Difference will become not disunion but routes and journeys towards the common goal which a Christian congregation will define for itself. In this constant process of working out and of dialogue, statements of core values may emerge, as will some discussion of what are the key Christian values we all share and on which we then build as we apply principles to the pragmatism of everyday life.

Team learning will be a cumulative bonus for the integrated congregation. The interaction of believers will produce an intelligence for the group or team which will exceed the intelligence of any of the individuals within it. The joint wisdom stemming from memory and open dialogue might well be a guidepost for how secure individuals are willing to suspend their own assumptions in order to be willing to think together.

Much has been said about building a shared vision around all the willing members of the congregation. But a vision without the systems to put it in place is no more than a lovely picture. The learning congregation will be concerned about the who and the how so that pathways are built so that the workers on the journey through a particular task are enabled and supported as they carry out their tasks.

7. Celebrate your achievements
Celebration is a natural way of expressing community and achievement.

Many of the most strikingly memorable pictures from the life of Jesus are the times when he eats a celebratory meal – at a wedding, with the tax-gatherers, in the Upper Room. The picture which he often gives of the Kingdom of Heaven is that of a great banquet. Congregations which have shared much together and gone through agonies may well say 'It was terrible in those meetings – but how we laughed together'. Anguishes as well as achievements must be celebrated. Religion and worship must have a real element of truthfulness and joy in them.

Modesty and humility sometimes hold us back from celebrating because we think that we are boasting, or even that we have done things only by our own efforts. Celebrations are a way of saying 'Thank you' to hard-working helpers and to God. Worship which is too inhibited is as dangerous as worship which is ecstatic in its uncontrolled exuberance.

When congregations work well we need just to thank God. We really can give thanks for all the learning, resources and wisdom now available to help us in our attempts to survive and to understand the great privilege of membership in a congregation. Without the understanding and support of others in an intimate group how else can we be saved from our worst selves and encouraged towards becoming the people in community that God wills us to be?

New-shape congregations

From what we have explored together I come with a real sense of excitement to look for hints and rumours of 'new-shape' congregations. Many of their characteristics already exist, we have only to recognize and acknowledge them. Others can come because we have developed a definite will to listen to local needs and to encourage and affirm innovation. We also have a genuine understanding of the problems and responsibilities which will come to those who are called into positions of leadership in new-style congregations and renewed denominations.

1. Local worship centres
People want to go to church in human-sized units.

In the main, people still want to go to a church which is close to where they live. This means that there is a future for the small church. It means that, for most people in the future, it will be more important to have a church in their local community than to travel to attend one of their original denomination. To be able to take your children to church and to meet friends you socialize with or meet in other local activities will continue to be important.

In order to maintain a local presence, community members will combine to 'save' their local church. Support for the building already has little connection with regular attendance. A building in a local community may well be managed by local people who will later choose to become church officers. Because there is a proprietorial sense of ownership for the building, though not always based in fact, it will be possible to raise large sums of money to maintain the building. It will almost certainly have a kitchen in it and will be used for concerts and other cultural events. It may even have toilets!

Local worship centres cannot have their own resident stipendiary clergy. Services will be taken by a range of authorized people. Non-stipendiary clergy will take a more prominent liturgical role alongside their being valued more for their secular priesthood. Some early retired or just retired clergy will be used to give time in exchange for occupancy of the clergy house. Stipendiary clergy will have the mini-episcopal role of oversight and will 'manage' a cluster of congregations.

2. Larger and smaller units

A natural consequence of local congregational strength is that larger and smaller units will characterize the church of the future.

Even the local unit will devolve its activities. The group meeting in a house or small public room will be the place where the Christian faith is developed. Groups will meet to accompany enquirers, to plan liturgies and to raise money to care for buildings. These groups will be much more informal than the structured committee system of organization. This method has been bankrupted by its inability to deliver a speedy and effective management system. It has also attracted a particular kind of person and culture which, at its most ridiculed, can be said to be made up of time-wasters or those who appear to have an endless fascination for detail.

The new-shape congregation will trust those with particular responsibilities to get on with the job. Congregationalism will not take over. It is of the essence of the church that it does not live for itself but knows that it is part of a wider whole. Congregations will either continue to be in their denominational grouping of Deanery or Circuit or they will want to recognize that their Christian presence is defined by geography. Congregations will group themselves according to the configuration of main roads or of canal drainage in the Fens or of hills in the Dales. Such geographical identity requires an ecumenical dimension for co-operation, mission and for the strategic maintenance of buildings. The nowadays unfortunately named Clergy Fraternal will be a place where clergy study together and where they think strategically. An already discerned lowering of denominational allegiance might mean that the area 'Churches Together Council' gains prominence. The lay training courses, missions and strategic planning for appointments can be done more effectively at this level. If denominational structures appear to prevent this area co-operation, it is those structures which should be questioned, and not the emergent local collaboration.

Smaller congregations will come together for uplifting services on specially designed occasions. I often think that God has given us fifth Sundays in the month just for this.

3. A new place for the clergy

In such exciting and innovative times there is absolutely no need for the clergy to feel insecure or undermined.

My look at history tells me that the generation of church restructuring following social and economic change is among the most interesting times to be a minister. We are in such days and there are new key tasks for the ordained to undertake. The laity in the congregations already want their ministers to be engaged in such activities.

- *A Holy Priesthood.* Whatever the denomination and its theological views about priesthood, congregations want their ministers to reflect the spirituality of their beliefs. Clergy are who they are, with the privileged position they have, because they have been called to represent God in particular ways. In times when there is a clear thirst for a developed spirituality among churchgoers and many non-churchgoers alike, the minister needs to be a person who says their prayers and who can help others to say theirs. Local communities want a man or woman of God among them who will bring another dimension to their hopes, fears and celebrations.
- *A teacher and inspirer.* The minister, an expensive asset in any denomination, will be expected to 'know their stuff'. Clergy will be required to have some teaching skills themselves in one or more areas of the Faith. They will also be the trainer and supporter of the trainers as lay people take the responsibility for the life of the local church. In an age where more and more people do not know the Christian story, there will be an increasing need for the best scholarship and most accessible learning methods to be available. For many Christian communities the minister is 'the holder of the vision'. While not requiring a race of total extroverts, congregations do need their minister to be a person who believes in the task they share together and who lifts them with the bigger picture.
- *Organizer and manager.* Clergy are given a particular organizational role in the local church. As local units are sustained by local people, the clergy will require a new range of skills. These will be in the area of managing groups of congregations. The skills are quite different from those traditionally used to pastor and organize one local congregation.

Ministers do not need to sneer at words like organization and management as if they only belong to the cold and impersonal world of cut-throat business and high finance. Good organization is tremendously pastoral. Training and in-service training will be a constant requirement for the minister with responsibility for the wider cluster of congregations.

4. Responsible financing
It will cost more and more to run the church of the future.

The days are over when church things can be done on the cheap. Clergy need to be paid and housed at a similar standard to that of other trained professionals. This has always been a controversial topic. If clergy are required to make sacrifices for their work, then they need to be free to choose in which areas these will be. The days of imposed poverty for the clergyman or woman, partner and their children are over. Acceptance of this has serious financial implications.

Given the choice, a congregation will choose to keep its building rather than its clergyman. To accept the responsibility of a church building, often of a special historic nature, is to take on an enormous commitment. Inadequate and expensive buildings cannot be kept on for worship by the few. Buildings in the wrong places need to be declared redundant. A denomination which can demonstrate that it is acting responsibly with its finances and over the use of its buildings will stand a much greater chance of gaining community support and grant aid.

5. New ways of working together
Clergy and laity in the newly shaped congregation will have discovered new ways of working together.

Collaboration still has for many the wartime overtones of working with the enemy. Collaboration within the churches today has to speak of new ways of sharing in a common vision and its consequent tasks. My shape for the new church is a pattern of interlocking circles, not a ladder or pyramid. Churches have not always followed their societies in every respect. The one significant area in which the churches can be formative, if not prophetic, is in the methods their members can discover for working together. Many communities are fragmented and divided by class and racial rivalry. Christian communities demonstrate or reflect little of this. They exist so that people from different groups and backgrounds can come together to share a common belief about the nature of creation and how men and women, women and men, with God as their guide, can work with one another. A congregation not committed to these beliefs as its inspiration does not deserve to survive. A congregation fired by these common collaborative experiences cannot fail to reflect the personality of the God who has chosen to work with us and to shape us into the Body of Christ on earth. Understanding congregations are the life-blood of that body.

Note

1   I have in mind here especially the formative writing of Peter Senge in *The Fifth Discipline*, where he describes five vital characteristics which build organizations – systems thinking, personal mastery, mental models, building shared vision and team learning (see page 115). This also compares with the eight characteristics of Peters and Waterman in their *In Search of Excellence* – bias for action, close to the customer, autonomy and entrepreneurship, productivity through people, stick to the knitting, simple form and lean staff, simultaneous loose-tight properties.

Bibliography

Michael Adie, *Held Together: An Exploration of Coherence* (London: Darton, Longman and Todd, 1997).

Gerald A. Arbuckle, *Refounding the Church: Dissent for Leadership* (London: Cassell (Geoffrey Chapman), 1993).

Paul Avis, *Authority, Leadership and Conflict in the Church* (London: Cassell (Mowbray), 1992).

Peter Ball, *Adult Way to Faith* (London: Cassell (Mowbray), 1992).

Peter Berger, *The Social Reality of Religion* (London: Faber & Faber, 1969; Penguin University Books, 1973).

Board for Mission, *Church of England: A Time for Sharing* (London: Church House Publishing, 1995).

Lord Bridge, *Synodical Government in the Church of England* (London: Church House Publishing, 1997).

Emil Brunner, *Our Faith* (London: SCM, 1936 – reprints to 1962).

Wesley Carr, *The Priestlike Task: A Model for Training and Developing the Church's Ministry* (London: SPCK, 1985).

David Clark (ed.), *Changing World, Unchanging Church?: An Agenda for Christians in Public Life* (London: Cassell (Mowbray), 1997).

Keith Clements, *Lovers of Discord: Twentieth Century Theological Controversies in England* (London: SPCK, 1988).

David Cormack, *Team Spirit: People Working with People* (London: MARC/Kingsway Publications, 1987).

Yvonne Craig, *Learning for Life: A Handbook of Adult Religious Education* (London: Cassell (Mowbray), 1994).

Peter Croft (ed.), *The Collaborative Church* (Barnsley: One for Christian Renewal, 1979).

Peter Croft, *A Primer for Teams* (Loughborough: One for Christian Renewal, 1979).

Thomas Downs, *The Parish as a Learning Community: Modeling for Parish and Adult Growth* (New York, Toronto: Paulist Press, 1979).

Peter Drucker, *The Age of Discontinuity: Guidelines to Our Changing Society* (London: Pan Books, 1968).

Avery Dulles, *Models of the Church: A Critical Assessment of the Church in All Its Aspects* (Dublin: Gill & Macmillan, revised edition, 1987).

Kevin Eastell, *Appointed for Growth: A Handbook of Ministry Development and Appraisal* (London: Cassell (Mowbray), 1994).

Giles Ecclestone (ed.), *The Parish Church?: Explorations in the Relationship of the Church and the World* (London: Mowbray/The Grubb Institute, 1988).

Leslie Francis and Paul Richter, *Gone but Not Forgotten: Church Leaving and Returning* (London: Darton, Longman and Todd, 1998).

Paulo Freire, *Pedagogy of the Oppressed* (London: Sheed & Ward, 1972; Penguin, 1972).

General Synod of the Church of England, *Breaking New Ground: Church Planting in the Church of England* (London: Church House Publishing, 1994).

Eliyahu Goldratt and Jeff Cox, *The Goal* (London: Gower Publishing, 1984).

Tim Gorringe, *Alan Ecclestone: Priest as Revolutionary* (Sheffield: Cairns Publications, 1994).

Laurie Green, *Let's Do Theology: A Pastoral Cycle Resource Book* (London: Cassell (Mowbray), 1990).

Robin Greenwood, *Transforming Priesthood: A New Theology of Mission and Ministry* (London: SPCK, 1994).

Robin Greenwood, *Practising Community: The Task of the Local Church* (London: SPCK, 1996).

John Habgood, *Faith and Uncertainty* (London: Darton, Longman and Todd, 1997).

Charles Handy, *Understanding Organisations* (London: Penguin Books, 4th edition, 1993).

Charles Handy, *The Empty Raincoat: Making Sense of the Future* (London: Hutchinson, 1994).

John Harvey-Jones, *Making It Happen: Reflections on Leadership* (London: Collins, 1988).

Adrian Hastings, *The Shaping of Prophecy: Passion, Perception and Practicality* (London: Cassell (Geoffrey Chapman), 1995).

Richard Higginson, *Transforming Leadership: A Christian Approach to Management* (London: SPCK, 1996).

Mike Hudson, *Managing Without Profit: The Art of Managing Third-sector Organisations* (London: Penguin, 1995).

George Lovell, *The Church and Community Development* (London: Grail/Chester House Publications for Avec 1972, with revisions 1980 and 1992).

George Lovell, *Analysis and Design* (London: Burns & Oates 1994).

George Lovell and Catherine Widdicombe, *Churches and Communities: An Approach to Development in the Local Church* (London: Search Press, 1978 and 1986).

Jeremy Martineau, *The Vicar Is Leaving* (Arthur Rank Centre, 1998).

Christopher Meakin, *'The Same but Different': The Relationship Between Unity and Diversity in the Theological Ecumenism of Yves Congar* (Lund: Studia Theologica Lundensia 50, Lund University Press, 1995).

Ann Morisy, *Beyond the Good Samaritan: Community Ministry and Mission* (London: Cassell (Mowbray), 1997).

John Nelson (ed.) *Managing and Leading: Challenging Questions for the Churches* (London: Canterbury Press for MODEM, 1988).

John Nelson (ed.), *Management and Ministry: Appreciating Contemporary Issues* (London: Canterbury Press for MODEM, 1996).

Stephen Pattinson, *The Faith of the Managers: When Management Becomes Religion* (London: Cassell, 1997).

Thomas J. Peters, *Liberation Management: Necessary Disorganization for the Nanosecond Nineties* (New York: Alfred A. Knopf, 1992).

Thomas J. Peters and Robert H. Waterman, *In Search of Excellence: Lessons from America's Best-run Companies* (New York: Harper & Row, 1982).

Stephen Platten, Graham James and Andrew Chandler, *New Soundings: Essays on Developing Tradition* (London: Darton, Longman and Todd, 1997).

Bruce Reed, *The Dynamics of Religion: Process and Movement in Christian Churches* (London: Darton, Longman and Todd, 1978).

Donald Reeves, *Down to Earth: A New Vision for the Church* (London: Cassell (Mowbray), 1997).

Peter Rudge, *Order and Disorder in Organisations* (Australia for CORAT, 1990).

Edward Schillebeeckx, *Ministry: A Case for Change* (London: SCM, 1981).

Michael Turnbull (Chair), *Working as One Body: The Report of the Archbishops' Commission on the Organisation of the Church of England* (London: Church House Publishing, 1995).

Peter C. Wagner, *Leading Your Church to Growth* (London: MARC Europe, 1984).

Robert Warren, *Building Missionary Congregations* (London: Church House Publishing, 1995).

Useful addresses

Adult Catechumenate Network, c/o Canon Peter Ball, Whittonedge, Whittonditch Road, Ramsbury, Marlborough, Wilts SN8 2PX.

The Alban Institute, 7315 Wisconsin Ave, Suite 1250W, Bethesda, MD 20814-3211, USA.

British Church Growth Association, The Park, Moggerhanger, Beds MK44 3RW.

The Edward King Institute for Ministry Development, c/o Church House, Churchyard, Hitchin, Herts SG5 1HP.

MODEM, c/o Mr Peter Bates, Carselands, Woodmancote, Henfield, W. Sussex BN5 9SS.

Index